The Everlasting
Answer—
Love

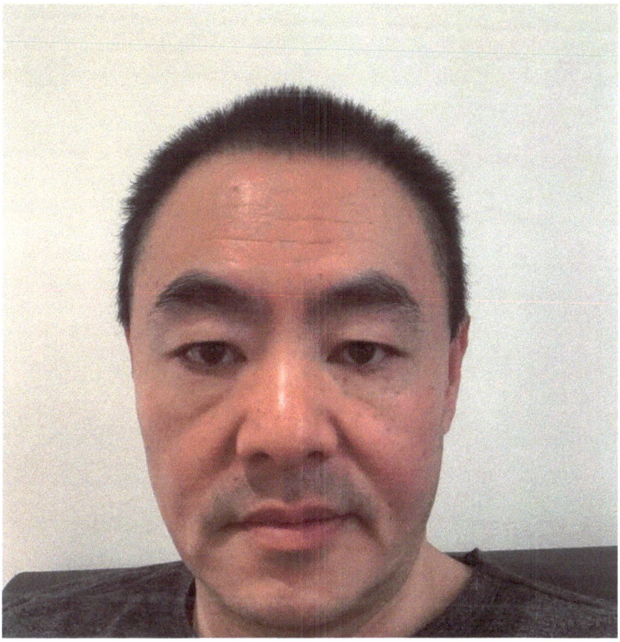

Spirit Guide

The Eastern Sage arrives

PROLOGUE

Heaven is more real than the human world, for the suffering here is temporary, whereas Heaven's light and joy are everlasting and infinite. Embrace the hardships of this human world. Face whatever you are experiencing now with the peaceful clarity of someone at the end of life. Forgive the conflicts of your present reality with a heart that has released its burdens and holds only warmth.

A practitioner belongs to Heaven, for only Heaven is real. Everything we experience in this lifetime—whether right or wrong, good or evil, joy or suffering—is a "karmic" realm arising from our inner attachments. When the heart lets go of its attachments, the outer cycle of "karmic cause and effect" can be resolved.

When the sense of self dissolves into inner forgiveness,

the original nature of Life awakens. Pure, everlasting, blissful Heaven will descend into this world through your body and mind. In that Heaven, all suffering is met with compassion and resolved; all sorrow and pain are healed; every trace of despair and death dissolves in the Light. Infinite Life brings infinite joy, and boundless Light gives rise to limitless hope.

Hope is the Light of Heaven.

If sentient beings hear the Truth, turn inward to contemplate body and mind, and awaken to the mind's original nature, then "the dream of birth and death dissolves, and mountains, rivers, and the great earth leave not an inch of ground."

As the soul awakens, the deluded tendencies accumulated over countless lifetimes that form the body, mind, and consciousness dissolve.

Manifestations of "physical illness" in the human world, as an expression of inner guilt meeting outer karmic forces, will be relieved. Sickness recedes, and healing and recovery unfold.

All these miraculous cases are really the result of the patients' own inner self-healing.

They are not miracles where the Truth directly intervenes to save a life or cure a disease.

The Truth clears away the confusion in people's minds; it does not seek to change their material living conditions.

The Truth only awakens the light deep within the soul; it does not alter one's external circumstances of life.

It is the hearts of sentient beings, embracing The Truth with faith,

that through spiritual awakening are transformed from within and thus bring physical healing.

It is the change in their own hearts that changes their destiny.

May all under heaven hear the Truth, begin by transforming their hearts, and thereby change the course of their lives.

CONTENTS

Parent-Child Relationship

A Harmonious Family

Depression

Recovery from Critical Illness

Rebirth in Love

Blessing and Merit

Expel a Spirit

Parent-Child Relationship

Overindulgence Can Stifle a Child's Ability to Survive

Student: This afternoon, my daughter sent me an article, part of which reads:

I have always been very obedient to my parents. If I buy something they don't like, I feel an overwhelming sense of guilt, as if I've violated morality and rules. It's not a big deal, really, but for someone like me, who has listened to my parents all my life, it feels like a huge psychological burden.

In the end, with my friends' encouragement, I went ahead and bought what I wanted, hahaha. Now, the more I look at it, the more I love it. But when I was buying it, I felt incredibly uncomfortable, like my heart was being torn apart. Not because of the money, but because I didn't follow my dad's advice. For twenty years, I've always followed their choices, so it felt like I was committing a crime, hahaha...

Then I thought, I want to make my own choice, just this once. Even if I end up regretting it, that's okay. I spent my own money on something I love, so what? If I end up not liking it in the future, if I feel like I made a bad choice, I can simply go back to listening to my parents next time. I don't have to keep living under the shadow of my childhood. So I made up my mind and bought it. Now, I feel really happy! I hope that those who feel the same way can also have the courage to buy what they truly want. As long as it doesn't go against important principles, you should always follow your heart! Forgive yourself for feeling guilty about not listening to your parents when making a purchase! It really helps. Just remind yourself: *It's just a purchase, just a difference in taste. Buy what you like!*

Master: Seeing your daughter's inner struggle, I can infer that as parents, your love has been overly controlling. It's really lucky for her that she's reached twenty without developing depression. Children need to form their own opinions, their own minds, their own thoughts and beliefs. Parents do not have the right to command them, and ideally should not even offer advice. Let them stumble, hit walls, suffer, and fail. Let them experience failure and fear. When a child's soul has endured enough hardships and the grind of reality, they will naturally develop a sense of self-protection. Their soul will then cultivate a rational and resilient inner strength. That's the right time for parents to step in and offer the support, emotional or material, that their child really needs. You cannot live your child's life for her. You will both one day leave her, and she is destined to face this cruel world alone.

Instead of raising her to be a fragile sapling with no survival skills, only to leave her alone to face the world's darkness and cruelty, why not let her experience hardship while you're still here to guide and support her? A heart that has known wounds is the only kind that can grow to be truly strong, clear, wise, and emotionally healthy. Parents who truly love their child would never let their own sense of insecurity lead them to overindulge the child to the point of stifling her ability to survive.

Bless your daughter. May she live independently, purely, and brightly.

Raising a child should be grounded in two key principles: First, self-discipline: teach a child to be mindful of their words and actions and to be considerate of others. Second, forgiveness: nurture the kindness in their heart. This is what builds a healthy, optimistic, and positive outlook.

TO LOVE A CHILD IS TO GIVE HER SECURITY AND COMPLETE FREEDOM

When it comes to raising a child, there is a clear bottom line: gambling, drugs, and pornography must never be touched, not even considered. Beyond that, whatever path you choose is entirely up to you. If you want to pick up trash to make a living, I'll support you. If you want to learn foot massage and serve others, I'll support you. If you want to sing on the streets for money, I'll be there to cheer you on. If you are willing to endure hardships and dedicate yourself to studying, I'll support you at all costs. In short, your life is your own to decide. Whatever choices you make, you must bear the consequences. Don't be afraid of failure. Failure is normal; success is rare. As long as you give it your all and have no regrets, your life will be full.

Everyone gets older. Looking back on my life now that I'm past 50, all the glory, wealth, attention, and praise of youth seem like fleeting clouds. What truly remains as one's own life memory is simply the journey of wholeheartedly devoting oneself to the things one genuinely wishes to do. This journey, marked by sincere, wholehearted effort, is the only thing that truly belongs to us. It is the clearest proof that we have truly lived.

If you live only to win society's approval and meet others' expectations, then that life belongs to them. You are not really living your own life. You've turned your existence into a performance, acting for the admiration, respect, praise, and accolades of others. When you grow old and weak, and the world forgets the role you once played, you may realize that your life felt pitiful, empty, and meaningless, because you never truly lived from your heart, nor burned your life's energy to fulfill your own true wishes.

In the end, that life, however glorious in the eyes of others, was just a walking shadow, empty of a true soul.

The core of educating a child is unconditional love and support. What is love? It is understanding, empathy, warmth without any conditions attached. What is support? It is giving everything you can unconditionally when she needs help, but never imposing any opinions or beliefs on the child in the name of authority. A child who willingly learns from books and turns that knowledge into life experience will grow to be confident, bright, discerning, insightful, courageous, and strong. What parents need to do is simply provide an ever-present "safety net" for their child, so that when she falls from the heights of her ideals, she can be supported with warm love and material means, to heal her wounds and come back stronger.

To love a child is to give her security and complete freedom.

THE BALANCE BETWEEN LOVE AND DISCIPLINE

Student: I've just begun to let go of family attachments. The road is long, but my resolve is firm. I have the determination and confidence to release my hold on family.

Vow: From this moment on, I am a monastic at heart, though living in the world. I will earnestly practice forgiveness, dissolve the self, and follow my Master on the path home. (Excerpt)

Master: Don't go to extremes. Disciplining children is the responsibility of the parents, and it must be done well; otherwise, you're not worthy of being a parent. When I talk about "letting go," I mean that, on the solid foundation of raising and guiding your child, you shouldn't form rigid, outcome-based "expectations" for them. That is, don't treat your child's education as a means to a goal. Rather than demanding a certain score, accept that doing their best is what truly matters. Don't insist they must get into a top university, or anything less is a failure. These kinds of specific, goal-oriented expectations suppress a child's spirit and can lead to depression. By the time your child's soul is sick and you are crying in regret, it will be too late.

I know a real case, people I'm acquainted with. Both parents are professors at Ivy League schools. Their child was a high-achiever from a young age and was later accepted to Columbia, one of the top Ivies . Once enrolled, after years of being outstanding, the child had developed an extremely high standard for himself. But under the strain of competing with top students globally, he could not cope with feelings of failure and took his own life.

As a parent, how would you feel in the face of such an ending?

Would you rather have a child at Harvard living on the edge of suicide, or a child with a simple job but a happy and healthy mind?

Another example: a mother with a successful career, is a senior executive at Pf* company. Her daughter was equally outstanding, always top of her class, and even won first place in the state for swimming. She was definitely on track for Harvard or Yale.

In the U.S., Asian females are often favored, while Asian males face more discrimination. For whatever reason, white Americans tend to be more accepting and kinder towards Asian women. She had everything needed to get into Harvard, Yale, or Stanford. However, years of academic stress damaged her health. She developed depression, dropped out of school, and now stays at home, thinking about suicide every day.

The parents can't do anything else, and they stay with her every day.

Your child might be average, but at least their spirit is well, isn't that what truly matters?

Have you ever really experienced what it's like when a child is sick? Even a simple cold or fever can leave you anxious and sleepless for a week, completely exhausted. But if your child becomes depressed or wants to hurt themselves, then all your hard work, success, luxury, and dreams for their future become meaningless.

Give your child a warm and safe home. Give your child a love that never changes. Give your child a promise of support

No blame, no rejection;
Just forgiveness and warmth;
Just acceptance and love.

and a path to fall back on. Let them face their own life. Discipline them, but don't force them. Reason with them, but never scold them. Do not impose your specific expectations on them. Let them choose their own goals, walk their own path, and learn to accept whatever comes from those choices.

Let your child fall. After being hurt a few times, they will come to realize that no one can be injured on their behalf, and that their pain does not transfer to others. Instinctively, they will begin to avoid paths that lead to suffering.

Love and discipline, both are essential.

Cases

FROM "STEPMOTHER" TO A "SISTER" ONE CAN SHARE EVERYTHING WITH

I got married at twenty-one and soon after had a daughter. But her arrival brought a lot of pain with it.

Less than a month after my daughter was born, my mother-in-law took her to a fortune teller. Back then, I had no judgment of my own and was completely ruled by fear. I just believed whatever my mother-in-law said.

The fortune teller said my daughter would bring misfortune to my side of the family and that she shouldn't call us "Mom" and "Dad," but instead call me "Teacher Zhou." Since I happened to be a kindergarten teacher, I went along with it.

From that point, "Teacher Zhou" treated her own daughter with growing harshness. Whenever something didn't go my way, I would explode in anger, yelling at her so severely that she fainted multiple times. What hurts me most now is that I never thought I was doing anything wrong. I showed no motherly love, not even a little. Even during the postpartum period, I could heartlessly let her cry for half an hour without feeling any pain or compassion.

When my daughter was nine, she started having frequent stomachaches, and they just got worse and worse. It became so bad that she sometimes couldn't attend school. I always thought she was faking it, so I'd scream awful things at her. Scenes of conflict between us became a regular occurrence at home.

Driven by superstition, I visited a so-called "living Buddha," who claimed my daughter would not live past ten unless I performed special rituals. It was devastating. I couldn't take it anymore. But still, I forced myself to endure it. Filled with fear, I chose to continue down that obsessive path. I spent a fortune on it, but my daughter didn't get any better.

My mother-in-law's relatives used to say I must have been a stepmother, because no real mother would be so cruel. And for over ten years, I took out all my frustration, anger, and unhappiness on my daughter, because she was just a child, and I didn't dare direct it at any adults.

Things grew worse in middle school. We often yelled and exchanged harsh words. Sometimes, to cope with her pain, she would run away from home or cut her arms. She also frequently suffered from severe mouth ulcers and recurrent fevers caused by throat inflammation, and sometimes it was so bad that even swallowing became difficult. We took her to a psychologist and had her checked at the hospital. She was diagnosed with depression, but the medication didn't seem to help much.

After one especially bad fight, she took more than a dozen antidepressant pills in two separate doses over four hours. We were at work when it happened and only discovered what she had done after we returned home. We rushed her to the hospital to have her stomach pumped. Thankfully, there were no serious consequences.

In 2021, I encountered Master's Teachings. At that time, my daughter was in middle school. Slowly, we started to see changes. We still argued, but it happened less and less often. Following each one, I worked on forgiving both of us, often crying as I navigated those difficult emotions.

During that time, recording of *Dream*[1] played nonstop in my daughter's room, 24 hours a day. She would often lower the volume, but I would gently turn it back up because I firmly believed, at the time, that hearing Master's voice was essential for her healing.

Later on, my daughter gradually stopped resisting. I started sending her short passages from Master's Teachings now and then, and she began responding with brief acknowledgments like "OK" or "Sure." At night, she even began playing the audio aloud. I would share with her stories of fellow practitioners and their transformations, and she started to enjoy listening more and more. Sometimes she would even chat with me about it.

It was a hard road, but every step was worth it, and it's brought me so much happiness.

---

1 *Dream* reveals, through the very essence of He, that all sentient beings have never been separate from Him. It reintroduces beings to their original self—the one they truly are Life. It illuminates the paths by which souls of different ranks return to Him. It is the restoration of His Wisdom; it is His forgiveness that dispels estrangement. It is the lifelong discipline of cultivation on the path of awakening, and the Dharma Protector that guards the soul.

After studying Master's Teachings, I came to realize that I truly love my daughter. But at the same time, my heart was also filled with so much guilt and remorse that I felt completely unworthy of being her mother. When we moved into our own place, separate from my mother-in-law, I also committed to working on myself. I gradually started to break down the emotional walls I had built and slowly loosened the grip that guilt had on me.

I know I made terrible mistakes and that I need to make amends, but I also see that staying stuck in self-blame doesn't help anyone. Doing so would not help my daughter, but it would only make things worse for both of us.

I remember Master once said: *Praise your child even if there's nothing specific to praise, just say something like, "You have such fair skin. You're so pretty."*

So I did just that and said, "Sweetheart, your skin is so nice and you look beautiful!"

One day, when she got up for breakfast, I sincerely said, "Sweetheart, you actually got up and had breakfast today, and

Love that comes from the soul can warm a child's heart. A healthy and pure heart is the true foundation for a well-rounded personality.

that's awesome!"

And so, bit by bit, I made a consistent effort to find new reasons to compliment her.

If my daughter did something that upset me, I would try to see it from her side and really work to understand her feelings. Over time, things gradually got better. Now, I can understand and empathize with her without even trying.

So how did I learn to love her? Whenever I'm clear-minded and at peace inside, I remind myself: "I love my daughter. I'm a good mother. My daughter doesn't resent me; in fact, she loves me as well."

In our day-to-day life, I do my best to attend to her small requests so she can feel my love. Over time, we became like sisters and we talked about everything, and our bond grew stronger and stronger. We might have minor disagreements now and then, but we always make up within minutes. Neither of us holds a grudge, and she often opens up to me and shares what's on her mind.

Now, there are basically no more arguments. Even if there's something unpleasant, we're able to express it calmly in the moment and let it go right away. We don't bottle things up until they explode anymore, like we used to.

At present, my daughter is positive and optimistic in her mindset. She's highly motivated in her studies, and even when she doesn't feel well physically, she still pushes through. She has stopped hurting herself and has started taking a real interest in her own well-being.

What makes me happiest is seeing the complete change in how she looks: her skin glows,her eyes are bright, and she has so much more energy. In the past, her face was pale, her eyes looked vacant, she had constant nightmares, and could barely drag herself out of bed. She was always exhausted and out of it. When she faced problems, she'd become incredibly angry and irritable, often withdrawing completely. Sometimes, she would lock herself in her room for days. But now, she's willing to listen to our advice. When I share Master's Teachings with her, she's open to them and even puts them into practice. I told her, "You need to learn to forgive, accept, and love yourself. Real strength isn't about fighting against things but about learning to release them. Trust that Master cares for you, and don't hesitate to seek his guidance."

She replied: "Okay!"

Cases

THE DESPAIR AND REDEMPTION OF A SINGLE MOTHER

Ever since I was little, my parents had to work from dawn till dusk to support the family, so they were hardly ever home.I spent most of my childhood without my mother around, and growing up like that left me feeling pessimistic and fearful. I often imagined sad things and didn't know what to say that would make others happy. As a result, people saw me as a withdrawn child, someone who didn't understand how to interact socially. I had very few friends. Often, the only strategy I felt I had to make people like me was to make fun of myself, using humor at my own expense to gain their approval and friendship. Inside, I had no sense of security. I was filled with fear, loneliness, and low self-esteem. In my parents' eyes, and in everyone else's, I was always a failure, someone who couldn't do anything right.

This feeling stayed with me from childhood all the way through college. Because I looked sweet and gentle on the outside, my appearance became the only thing I could show off to regain a bit of self-worth. But deep down, I was extremely insecure and fragile. I was a person with sky-high ambitions, yet I felt my destiny was as fragile as paper. I secretly hoped to find someone wealthy and live a good life, but life kept disappointing me.

My first marriage fell apart after I suffered several consecutive miscarriages, which led to infertility and a diagnosis of polycystic ovary syndrome (PCOS). As a result, I could no longer conceive, and I suddenly gained over 30 jin (around 15 kilograms), causing my body to become completely unrecognizable. The shallow confidence I'd built on my appearance vanished overnight, leaving behind a much deeper sense of worthlessness and a growing distrust of the world.

My first husband filed for divorce on the very day I had a miscarriage. I couldn't handle the double blow and developed obsessive-compulsive disorder (OCD) on top of my depression. Whenever it flared up, two opposing thoughts would battle in my mind. For example, if I walked by a river and saw a child, a sudden thought would pop into my head to push the child into the river and drown them. But my rational mind would tell me

I couldn't do that, while another thought would keep urging me to do it quickly. To control these bad thoughts, I'd resort to extreme measures like slapping myself repeatedly and banging my head against the wall, trying to stop those terrifying thoughts.

If only I had found the Master's Teachings back then and learned how to forgive, accept, and hold space for those painful thoughts and experiences, perhaps my child would have been spared so much suffering later. The regret is profound.

After my divorce in 2012, I began to explore Buddhism and entered the Buddhist path, but unfortunately, I was learning from a heterodox teaching. In 2014, heaven blessed me with a lovely child. During my pregnancy, I had very auspicious dreams. I used to be a superstitious person and believed that this child came to me as a result of my animal release practices and prayers, so I was convinced that he was extraordinary and came with a mission. This selfish attachment made me believe my child could single-handedly rescue me from my unhappy life and earn me the admiration and respect I had always craved. As a result, my personality split again: I sought attention by showing off my child, trying to fill the pain of my own failed life.

In 2016, when my child was just over one year old and had just learned to walk, I was studying a heterodox form of traditional culture. Following the teachings from *The First Lesson Between Father and Son Under Heaven*, I made my son, who was still wearing open-crotch pants, mop the floor, wipe tables, and do housework. Whenever he disobeyed me, I made him kneel as punishment and beat him with bamboo rulers. I bought several of these rulers online, hiding behind the idea of "traditional cultural education" to justify venting my own inner agony and hopelessness on him. At that time, my husband had no job, showed no ambition, and our family relied solely on me to earn a living. The pressure to survive was immense, and I got no emotional support from him, with him often being cold and indifferent. But because I had grown up timid and insecure, I dared not express my anger and kept suppressing it. Instead, I turned all my cruelty, pain, and despair toward my defenseless child. Whenever he did the smallest thing that upset me, I would feel my anger surge. My eyes would blaze, and the house would often ring with his cries of pain.

At that age, my child didn't understand anything at all, but I demanded he read my mind like an adult. Whenever he failed to do so, I would beat him brutally. Many times, thick bamboo sticks were broken, but my anger still wouldn't subside. Seeing him cry, gasp for air, and try to hide, I would feel overwhelming guilt and could only keep slapping myself in the face. Days like that happened almost every other day. Both my child and I were trapped in a living hell. I stubbornly convinced myself that without this harsh discipline, he would never succeed, never become someone I could show off with pride, and never somehow make up for my first husband leaving me because I couldn't conceive.

At that time, my heart was filled with malice, resentment, and anger. I felt like I was the most miserable person in the world and believed that everyone had wronged me. For nearly five years, I constantly had hallucinations of a giant python chasing me. In the second half of 2017, after watching an Indian movie about the Buddha's life, I felt immense joy and a deep sense of reverence for him. I made a vow to spread *The Life of the Buddha*, hoping to help more people come to know and revere him. In December 2017, through the karmic connection with *The Life of the Buddha*,I came to know a Dharma sister who followed Master's teachings. After hearing about my situation, she kindly mailed me Master's audio player and a book titled *Dream*.

From very first day I received Master's audio player, I began playing *Dream* on loop at home. Whether I understood it or not, I kept it playing continuously. Whenever I went out, I carried a portable player with me, listening to it through earphones on my way to and from work.

I carry heavy karmic burdens. For over two years after I started listening to the teachings, I faced repeated, serious health crises where I nearly died several times, all while my family was in turmoil. My depression relapsed. Although I had been studying Master's Teachings for over two years, I hadn't truly understood it. What I believed to be forgiveness was actually forcing myself to forgive the person who had hurt me externally, rather than forgiving the pain within myself. My efforts were superficial. I was still holding onto the belief that my task was to forgive someone else, forcing myself to act like a good person while avoiding the profound pain and despair I carried inside. As a result, even after more than two years, I still frequently lost my need to control of my emotions and beat my child. Each time, I was filled with guilt and agony afterward, and my heart remained full of hatred and resentment toward outside world.

In 2022, which was my fourth year of studying Master's Teachings, a series of recordings on "Forgiveness," including ones titled "Warming the Ego," was released. Around that time, I was going through another painful period: the father of my child had left us for someone else. Every day, I listened to Master's audios like *Warming the Ego* and *Forgiveness Guidance*, often crying as I listened. Then, suddenly, I realized I had been wrong all along. I finally saw that my pain did not originate from outside events; it was generated from within me. I had never truly forgiven myself, never truly entered my own heart to accept and embrace the pain that was there.

Because of that, all my suffering remained unacknowledged and misunderstood, repressed deep inside, and it would explode whenever I encountered triggering situations. I realized that real forgiveness, at its core, is about forgiving ourselves. It's about forgiving the part of us that sees the world through a lens of fear and that clings tightly to things because of that fear.

So I learned to stop defining myself. When painful memories

surfaced, I would visualize a warmer, more compassionate version of myself gently holding that pain and surrounding it with unconditional warmth and love. Just like comforting a newborn baby, I cradled all my suffering and despair in my arms, soothing, warming, understanding, and embracing the needs of my own heart. In that state of complete acceptance and embrace, I allowed my pain and despair to be released. I gradually realized that when rage welled up inside me, I could clearly see my own motives and emotions, and pulled myself back in time. The incidents of hitting my child slowly began to decrease. One day, my child told me, "I like the mom you are now. The mom you were before scared me." His words pierced my heart. Hearing those words, my heart ached deeply. While other children grew up receiving endless love and affection from their parents, mine had only ever faced my uncontrollable outbursts and beatings.

In the past year or so, I faced challenges no less difficult than those from years before, and they assailed me relentlessly from every aspect of life: the constant threat of losing my job, the looming risk of serious illness, and various issues with my child, including health concerns and social withdrawal. Yet I noticed that as I faced these difficulties, my inner experience has shifted. In the past, I would have asked, "Why is my life so difficult?" and felt I was cursed with bad luck. But now, I feel a deep sense of calm. I've come to understand that the root of my suffering does not lie in the external world. It is born from my own internal demands and my judgments of good and bad, right and wrong. Ultimately, all the suffering I endured grew from my own inner cravings and attachments.

As Master said, everything is just a replay of what has already occurred. So why try to change the dream or rewrite what has already been determined? When I learned to accept life without resisting or clinging to it, and when I began to see every hardship as a chance to test and deepen my practice, I started to treasure each challenge and respond with forgiveness, gratitude, and love. It was then that I unexpectedly understood: every difficulty we face is really a compassionate guide in disguise, leading us toward freedom from the cycle of birth and death.

I've come to realize that the most powerful teaching for my son comes when I accept and embrace my own attachments to the outside world, forgive my own desires and pain, release my anxieties for my child, courageously face my true self, and surrender to the natural flow of life. I stop chasing illusions and instead choose to walk beside my son with love and warmth, sharing Master's compassion so he feels truly loved and accepted for who he is.

My child is changing too, little by little. His wounded heart is slowly healing through love and warmth. I firmly believe that only love and acceptance can dissolve all barriers and pain.

A Harmonious Family

A FAMILY IS NOT A PLACE FOR REASONING

A family is where two souls, each with their own traits, temperaments, and edges, collide and merge. Within that intimate circle, mutual trust and never hurting each other's tender spots are the most basic forms of respect. You cannot change another person's inner experience, as it carries karmic impressions from countless past lives. They cannot change yours either. But you can find what brings you both joy, and do those things together. That is the core of building a family. Find harmony without demanding the other person be just like you. Don't expect them to absorb every part of who you are, and it's okay to keep a private space deep inside, something independent, free, and just for you. A couple

are meant to walk through life together. Don't force your views or preferences on each other, and respect the other's perspective, even when you disagree. But never try to force change upon them. As time passes and the initial passion fades, each person's distinct personality and deep-seated habits will fully unfold. For the rest of your lives together, what you'll need most is understanding, forgiveness, acceptance, empathy, and the warmth of trust. A family is not a place for reasoning, but a haven of safety and rest for the soul. Within it, a loved one is more like a dear friend, who accepts and forgives the other's imperfections with the warmth of trust and empathy. Only then can each person find in the other comfort for the heart, peace for the body and mind, and joy for the soul.

WHERE IS THIS MARRIAGE HEADED—CONTINUE OR PART WAYS?

Family conflicts are often the most complex because each side insists they're right, and it is difficult to discern the truth. I offer an approach to sorting out family issues: the person involved needs to reflect calmly. Never think while angry; wait until emotions settle, then objectively assess alone: what level of happiness do you truly feel when living with this person? If your happiness level in the marriage is above 80%, then your marriage is already very successful, and you should avoid looking for problems where none exists. But if it's only 60-70%, then living a single life would bring a similar sense of fulfillment. In that case, marriage might feel like an unnecessary compromise, since being married or single gives you about the same sense of personal fulfillment.

If it's below 60%, you should part ways as soon as you can, so you don't waste your life in endless pain, hurting both yourself and the other person.

Once you've calmly thought it through, you'll have a clearer idea of the path ahead. You can choose to continue life as it is, live together politely but with emotional distance, or decide to part ways.

First, if the happiness level between you two exceeds 80%, then your family is already happier than over 90% of families on earth, so what is there left to complain about? What's worth arguing over? Since you've chosen to spend your life with this person, and you'll still have to live together after the quarrel, what's the point of fighting in the first place?

A family should be a place for love, not for reasoning. If you truly love each other, why not forgive each other's occasional unreasonable behavior?

Second, if you compromise in a seemingly harmonious but emotionally distant way, like familiar strangers, there's even less reason to argue. Between strangers, mutual respect and boundaries are key; peaceful relations come from respecting and understanding each other. It's like encountering an unreasonable troublemaker on the street: "A moment of patience brings calm; a step back opens vast skies." There's no need to quarrel over trivial matters. Just as you wouldn't waste your breath reasoning with a street thug, trying to convince them to follow your views, so why make things harder for the family living under the same roof?

In the third scenario, there's even less reason for conflict. You've already decided to separate, and your paths in life are about to diverge. Part gracefully and amicably. Embody the virtues of a practitioner: forgive, pardon, and treat each other with kindness. Bid farewell with courtesy and respect, and embark on new journeys. Why resort to hostility, engaging in bitter clashes or deliberate harm, just to end this bond.

Please remember that the person you're gritting your teeth at right now is the same person who once moved you to tears, who swore heartfelt vows to you for a shared future, and who once declared without hesitation, "I must marry you." This is the person you once loved—the embodiment of your past romance, your faded youth, your original dreams, and all the hopes and longings you once pinned on them.

Hurting the person in front of you today is like betraying

your own past self. What's the point?

Forgive the person you resent, and also forgive the part of yourself that is trapped by that hatred. Set them free, and you will grant yourself a future unbound. Extend your former love blessings and prayers.

May the light of faith illuminate your soul.
May the warmth of the Divine accompany your life.

Never argue with the one you love, and never try to ease your own loneliness or fear by hurting someone else.

You are a soul beloved by the Divine.
You are meant to extend love to the world.

PARENTS STAY YOUNG WHEN THEY ARE NEEDED BY THEIR CHILDREN

Student: I love my mom more than anything, so deeply that it feels limitless. Yet, I often find that I lose my temper with her the most, and recently I've begun focusing on all her small imperfections. I keep lecturing her because she's spent her whole life being so frugal, never willing to spend a penny on herself, yet she's so incredibly generous with me, as if she'd give me the whole world if she could. But I don't even want that whole world from her. I want to give her the best of everything too, and that's where our clashes come from. Now, she's the only person who can really make me angry, because I care about her too much, because I ache for her too deeply. I always want to give her the best of everything, but she turns down whatever I offer her. Instead, she insists on giving me everything she has. Honestly speaking, she's pained by every penny I spend on her. When it comes to herself, she's painfully stingy with money, but if I crave a favorite snack, no matter how expensive, she'll buy it without even blinking—no

hesitation whatsoever.(Excerpt)

Master: Do not try to change elderly people's habits. For them, changing long-formed habits and beliefs is a form of suffering. Although I come from a family of high-ranking officials, my parents' salaries had to support my grandfather's and maternal grandfather's families, so our life was not affluent when I was young. The habits formed in my early years have led me to remain very frugal even today. The coat I am wearing now is still one I bought twenty years ago. This sense of frugality actually gives me a feeling of comfort and reassurance. You also should not refuse the love your elders offer you, as their giving is their way of asking for your love in return. Bringing happiness to those they love, is the greatest reward for the one who loves.

Therefore when I was back home in China, I'd go from being an independent man into a spoiled son. I was fed by others, clothed by others, and I never lifted a finger myself. I simply accept my parents' love, for I can see through their deepest motives. Parents, who are often accustomed to directing their children's lives, may impose their love in ways that feel controlling. And to make parents happy, I act out the part of the child they want me to be—the needy, dependent one who always relies on their care.

In this way, parents gain a "sense of value" through being needed and relied upon by their children.

This "sense of value" is deeply important for one's emotional well-being, and this is especially true for the elderly.

Because parents stay young when they are needed by their children.

Cases
FROM FIERCE QUARRELS TO HARMONY IN THE OWNER'S FAMILY

I used to own a fairly successful business, but it suddenly failed, and my income disappeared. Then my child fell ill with asthma and heart palpitations. Soon after, I also got sick. For years, I dared not go outside in any season; even in the peak of summer, I couldn't open the windows. The slightest breeze would give me splitting headaches and severe diarrhea. I lost a drastic amount of weight, becoming skeletal, and I developed severe depression, insomnia, and other issues; it felt like I was sick in every way possible. Eventually, my condition turned critical; both traditional Chinese and Western medicine were powerless, and I could only watch helplessly as my health kept getting worse.

After I became sick, I was gripped by intense fear, and I interpreted every new symptom as a sure sign of cancer. I became obsessed, searching on my phone day and night. The more I read, the more terrified I became, but I couldn't stop.

I'd scare myself so badly I'd lie awake crying all night. But the worst part was that no one in my family understood me. Instead, they just kept blaming me and attacking me, nonstop.

I can't go on anymore. I'm going to die. I was indescribably weak. I screamed and cried with what little strength I had left. I cried on the roadside, sobbed under my blankets, knelt on the floor, sat in despair, and felt completely overwhelmed with sorrow.

When I reached my lowest point and felt completely consumed by despair and helplessness, I found the Truth. Clinging to it like a drowning man to a lifeline, I started copying *Dream*, transcribing *The River of Life and Death*[1], copying every written resource, chanting the *Confession Scripture*, and committing *Dream* to memory. At first, my frail body couldn't handle even half an hour of copying. Gradually,

---

1 *The River of Life and Death* is a practitioner's definitive guide to realizing Budda's Dharma—a complete experiential path that transcends body-mind consciousness, awakens true nature, and meticulously documents the practitioner's journey from the ordinary realm to liberation from the "self" experience; from witnessing the unborn Truth within the spiritual realm, to restoring Reality through compassion, and embodying the solemnity of nirvana.

however, my stamina grew until I could copy for ten hours a day and even recite *Dream* eighty times in a single day.

Before I began practicing the Dharma, my family and I argued constantly for years, and the anger and resentment inside me never faded. Fights with my husband often ended with us hurling chairs at each other. My temper was so explosive that I yelled and made my child cry almost daily. I always looked down on my husband for only having a junior high school education. When we got married, his relatives said, "Marrying ** is your good fortune." I nodded along, but inside, I felt nothing but contempt—after all, I had always been a top student.

After I began studying the teachings, I clearly saw that regardless of a person's level of education, we are all merely ghosts awaiting death. I no longer envy anything in this worldly life. All I yearn for is to cultivate the utmost renunciation and devotion, to follow my Master in practice life after life, and to return home with my Master.

Before I started practicing, if a family member made a simple comment like, "You forgot to take out the trash," I'd

Forgiveness paves the way for compassionate understanding; through understanding comes release, and through release emerges freedom from the karmic bonds of past lives.

immediately fall apart. I would burst into tears and shout, "I've been sick for years, and you never understand how ill I really am! Don't you know I can't go out in the wind?!" Their single remark could reduce me to such anguish that my head throbbed unbearably, as if it were splitting apart.

After studying the Dharma, I forgave the grievances within my heart. After all, they weren't truly me. I came to understand and forgive them. Once I forgave, it felt as though nothing had ever happened. I realized then that suffering isn't inherently real. I understood that the "enemy" isn't outside of me. What I needed to forgive wasn't others, it was simply my own self, desperate for recognition and understanding, insisting on imposing my own views on others.

So when the same situation came up again, I responded calmly, almost playfully: "You're right, I didn't take the trash out. I wasn't feeling well." I dared to express myself without a hint of resentment. And miraculously, the family member who had been angry calmed down right away, no longer upset about the chore, as if nothing had happened. Instead, they called me adorable. Truly, the external world is merely a reflection of the inner self.

The power of the Truth allowed me to forgive my family completely and without reservation. My home has long since been filled with harmony. It turns out that all of this was purely my own karmic obstacle, having nothing to do with my family at all. From then on, the lingering resentment in my heart vanished without a trace. This is the redemption of the Divine. Where in humanity lies the capacity to forgive?

At a meal with my husband's relatives, I spoke from the heart and said with complete sincerity, "I'm so lucky to have married him. He's a deeply responsible man, devoted to his parents, loving to his wife and children, a man of true integrity." The disdain I'd once harbored for my husband vanished completely, replaced by genuine praise. As for my mother-in-law, my attitude shifted from superficial compliments to heartfelt admiration.

I love my family, but I no longer cling tightly to this affection and familial bond. I yearn for the Dharma, yearn to transcend the cycle of life and death. Only the Dharma can redeem me from samsara.

My father-in-law passed away unexpectedly two weeks ago after a fall, leaving us without a final word. He spent his life clinging to money, yet in the end, it all amounted to nothing. Just two days ago, a very wealthy friend, who had promised to visit my mother-in-law, died suddenly of a heart attack at just over 40. What use is wealth? Money can't solve the problem of life and death.

Before studying the Dharma, I was once paralyzed by my

fear of death. When I looked at my father-in-law's body, I suddenly realized that death was nothing to dread. The elderly man had passed away while listening to *Guidance*[1]. It meant a karmic bond had already been forged—he would surely continue his practice until liberation in the future.

What's truly terrifying isn't death, pain, or disaster. It's having the Dharma right in front of you and still refusing to believe in it or practice it. That is the real catastrophe.

1 *Guidance* recited by Master is a beacon of light from the Spirit Heaven, coming to receive and lead the departed. Within the audio abides the radiance, warmth, and grace of the True Divine. Though souls that have left this world differ in their habitual tendencies and delusive thoughts, the shared framework of the "five aggregates and six consciousness" that composes the soul is the same. The blossoming light of Spirit can penetrate the soul, and the deep peace carried within Life can deliver the soul into redemption.

Cases

Once obstinate and closed-off, he grew warm and gentle

My husband and I got married after knowing each other for less than three months. Our personalities and temperaments clash intensely, and we mutually believe the other was a hopeless case. Just a few words were enough to start a fight between us.

Let me give you an example. A few years ago, I wanted to visit Mount Putuo every year. One time, we were staying in a hotel room with the towering statue of the South Sea Guanyin right outside our window, yet we ended up having a furious argument inside the room. Another time, we were already on the opposite side of the sea but ended up not going at all because of yet another fight. I felt too ashamed to face the Bodhisattva's statue, thinking that even it would not want to see two such lowly and foolish people.

On one occasion, we screamed and hurled insults at each

other. He threw my Buddhist beads out of the car window and into the street. In the two or three years before I encountered the Truth, there was a day when, during a scuffle, I fell to the ground. He raised his foot high above my chest, though he didn't bring it down—but that overwhelming sense of humiliation nearly suffocated me. I had never been subjected to such disgrace; the shame felt as heavy as a mountain pressing down on me, and it was unbearable. And yet, I had nowhere to turn for solace or support.

No matter how we tried to make adjustments, life remained a chaotic mess. He wrote me a letter of commitment, and I suggested we have tea and talk once a week, or read a certain book together. We even came up with "penalty rules" for after we fought. I wrote letters to communicate with him, clearly telling him what I needed most when I lost emotional control... For the sake of our child, I really exhausted all my efforts over those years trying to make this family work. But no matter how we talked or how hard we tried to find solutions, it became clear that trying to change a stubborn adult using ordinary worldly methods is absolutely impossible.

In 2019, I was finally introduced to Master's Teachings. It

felt like a drowning person battling towering waves in a stormy sea who suddenly finds a lifebuoy, or like someone dying of thirst in the desert who suddenly catches sight of an oasis.

From then on, whenever I was in a bad mood, as long as he read a passage from Master's Teachings, no matter how out of control I was at that moment, my nerves would be soothed—almost instantly, as if I'd been injected with a sedative. The effect was immediate and obvious. We both found it truly miraculous.

I told him I hoped he'd focus entirely on studying Master's Teachings instead of spending time on standing meditation. When I said that, he got furious and shouted, "I'm not learning your stuff! I'd rather die!" So, I suggested he pick me up from work more often. As soon as we got in the car, I would play Master's audio teachings. At first, he was very resistant but didn't dare to speak out. Yet he gradually became more accepting. One year during the National Day holiday, when we got stuck in traffic, he actually said calmly, "It's okay. It's fine. The traffic jam is great, and it gives us more time to listen to the teachings."

The real turning point arrived during the first year of the pandemic. I was required to quarantine because I had traveled through Hubei Province, China. I was alone in a completely enclosed room with no windows. I have a touch of claustrophobia, and the whole floor was full of high-risk close contacts. I was terrified, and the only way I got through each day was by copying and listening to the teachings. I begged my husband, "I'm so scared. Can you and our son read *Dream* with me over the phone every day?" He agreed. The quarantine period lasted half a month. Then, one day, I suddenly sensed a new sincerity in his voice during our call; he was no longer just going through the motions. Hearing this, I was moved to tears.

After I got home from the quarantine hotel, he said, "At first, I was just reading with you to keep you company. But then, as I kept reading, I suddenly realized that it's really beautiful. Maybe I should memorize *Dream* too. I'll start copying it as well!" I sensed the sincerity behind his words, and once again, tears streamed down my face.

I did my part by offering him the camphorwood table, the brightest, most pleasant one in the house. And true to his word, he memorized *Dream* in just a few months.

Without noticing it, we started arguing less, and when we did, our fights were much milder. Once, while I was studying the Dharma, he quietly placed a cup of tea in front of me. In that moment, I could feel the gentleness, warmth, and approval he was offering, and it struck me that he seemed like a completely different person from the impatient and stubborn man he used to be.

One time, while he was giving our child a piano lesson, the room was filled with his loud voice, the child's crying, and the heavy thumping of keys. I felt anxious and on edge, but I restrained myself from intervening and starting a conflict. I kept my attention on my own heart, which felt tight and clenched. Leaning on my Master, I forgave that part of me, soothed it, and confessed to it. I said to that part of myself, "I will recite *Dream* once, and I pray that the merit of reciting it will be dedicated to you, hoping it will bring you some warmth." As I started reciting *Dream*, it felt like that part of me sensed my sincerity. Tears streamed down my face like water from an open tap, but at the same time, there was a sense of release, a feeling of lightness.

Forgiveness isn't about forcing yourself to "love." It's about forgiving the parts of yourself that you thought were "unforgivable," and once you do, all that's left is "love."

Another time, I was overwhelmed with grievance and anger because of something with my mother. I was too exhausted to confess, too hurt to forgive. I could only collapse onto the floor and cry. To my surprise, he told me he was starting to understand the pain I had carried from my relationship with my parents. He comforted me and urged me not to give up, encouraging me by saying that I had already improved tremendously.

He used to be unable to appreciate beauty or empathize with others. No matter how well we treated him in the past, we couldn't reach his heart. But now, our Master's Teachings, like nourishing rain and sweet dew, have awakened his heart and revived his capacity to feel. He has begun to open up, and his heart has become so much softer.

Sometimes, after just a few minutes of arguing with me, he would seem like a completely different person who is no longer so repulsive or hard to bear. Instead, he would calmly

comfort me, saying that he understood I was suffering, that my parents and sister didn't understand me, but he did. He told me he really admired me and gave me a big thumbs-up. He would also reflect on his own outbursts and apologize. Since he started studying *Dream*, he has truly made remarkable progress.

In my husband, in my parents and family, I see how the compassionate wisdom of the Dharma is gradually awakening love in all beings. At the same time, I reflect on my own harshness, my need to control, resentment, and contempt in my relationship with my husband, and I vow to change each and every one of these tendencies.

Cases
From Vanity and Arrogance to Selfless Gratitude

I did not grow up in a wealthy or luxurious home, but my parents adored me. My days were filled with music, calligraphy, chess, and painting, which shaped me into what many saw as a quintessential artistic young woman. Later, I taught Chinese literature and traditional culture at an elite private school, where both students and parents thought highly of me. All of these experiences made me emotionally sensitive, detail-oriented, somewhat vain and proud, and quite certain that I was always right.

And then there was him who was simple, honest, and not much of a talker, someone who didn't dwell on things or remember details. You can imagine how little attention he paid to my delicate, romantic, and sensitive nature, and how this affected my ego. When I tried to hint at things gently, he wouldn't understand or remember. When I thought about being more direct, my pride and vanity held me back and I didn't want to be that obvious. I secretly wished he could just read my mind.

For example, there was a time when I wanted him to buy me a gift. First, I bought presents for him and his family, then I dropped subtle hints, trying to nudge him indirectly. But he didn't get it, and I ended up feeling frustrated and upset. He noticed that I was unhappy, and after asking layer upon layer of questions, he finally realized that I had been hoping to receive a gift from him.

It wasn't until I began studying Master's Teachings that I truly understood: Every situation we face is here to awaken the qualities that belong to Heaven within our hearts. These situations may stir up many emotions, but most of them are rooted in fear, grasping, and self-protection. Our Master teaches us that what can truly dissolve fear is love, both the love we offer ourselves and the love we extend to others.

In the past, I hid behind a polished version of myself because I felt compelled to show only my best side. I often said one thing while feeling another, and living that way eventually exhausted me. But as I studied and practiced the teachings

If you're weighed down by suspicion, doubt, or resentment, and you choose to speak honestly about those feelings, you may find that the other person isn't actually the way you imagined, or the way your misunderstanding led you to believe. This is what we mean by "说破无毒" — when spoken honestly and without malice, expressing your true thoughts does no harm.

of my Master, I gradually began to open my heart. As the saying goes, "When spoken with honesty and without malice, expressing your true thoughts does no harm." I'm learning to let things unfold naturally, to express myself freely, to free my heart so I'm no longer bound by rigid moral judgments, because Heaven doesn't care about those things.

When we were in a relationship, I was in Zhuhai and he was in Tianjin. Most of the time, we could only communicate by phone. Later, when I was about to leave Zhuhai, my relatives, friends, and even school leaders all came to me with the same messages: "Don't give up your career for someone else. Don't keep giving without boundaries." I brushed their words aside, yet inside, old fears quietly rose to the surface. Just thinking about not having money, not having a nice place to live, losing a good job, being away from my parents, missing my familiar friends and warm environment, and not having a paycheck to spend on wellness, jewelry, clothes, or delicious food... Even though I knew all of it was like a dream that is insubstantial and fleeting, the fear still came rushing over me like a tidal wave. This huge wave of fear washed over me four or five times, until we got married.

I made a list of all the external things triggering my fear and worked through them one by one. I opened my heart to the love and care my husband and my in-laws were already offering me. Then, drawing on the strength of my faith, I began to warm, forgive, and release my fear. Over and over, I would separate from the fear, talk to it, hold it with warmth, and for give it. Again and again, I whispered: "I love you. I forgive you. I bless you." Little by little, that fear softened and faded like morning mist, and my heart grew light and free. Because in the end, only love can dissolve fear.

What he gives me may not always be what I want, but it is everything he has to offer. He is willing to give, to care for me, and to take on the responsibility for my future. I should cherish this kindness and learn to understand and accept him. As Master said:"If a man loves you this deeply and is willing to carry the weight of your life, then he is someone to whom you should offer the same deep gratitude you would show your parents."

Through extensive study and practice of the Dharma, the light and warmth of have gradually melted the coldness in my heart that had long been frozen in matters of love. Little by little, I learned to express my love to him. Gradually, I also learned to love myself, to love him in return, and to fully accept him as he is. From there, my love extended to his family and to the people around me. Often, the two of us would express to each other: "I'm grateful for you. I love you." I am committed to returning the warmth he's brought into my life. His heart grows more and more selfless through spiritual practice, and that is exactly what I strive to learn from him.

After we got married, I moved to Tianjin. Marriage came with a lot of daily chores and little things that really tested my patience. For example, I used to have meals at school, or my parents would cook for me, or I'd order takeout. Now, I had to cook for myself. I learned to wash clothes only in college, but now I had to share half the household duties. Before, I would go shopping from time to time, paint, do crafts, string beads, design and alter clothes, take care of my wellness, write poetry, all of these little joys and routines were suddenly disrupted. I didn't know anyone around me except my husband and family, and I even got lost when going out... My ego felt like crying and wanted to scream to the sky. But it's okay, because my higher self has faith, and where there is faith, there is light.

Since 2022, in the compassionate presence of Master, often just a simple phrase like "I forgive you, I love you, and I bless you", has carried profound power. It helps me uncover the underlying memories, fears, and motives of grasping or demanding, and when I offer forgiveness to those motives, the heaviness of the moment fades far more quickly than it once did. After forgiveness, a gentle sense of gratitude and softness often arises, which feels especially warm and soothing.

Sometimes, when something triggers me, I don't overthink it. I just turn to the Dharma right away. As I listen, my mind and heart settle for a moment, and as I continue reading, the tangled thoughts loosen and slip away, bringing a quiet sense of ease. As I copy Master's Teachings, a faint sense of peace and gentleness radiates from my spine. My mind becomes clear and serene. In that stillness, every stroke I make is filled with love; every line is like a ray of light, melting away hardened parts of myself and strengthening the life of my faith. How beautiful it is! Sometimes, I simply look up to Heaven and behold the love of the Divine. And before I know it, my habitual patterns and old experiences dissolve away naturally.

If it weren't for Master's Teachings, I might have remained a vain and restless soul, caught in the endless patterns of samsara who places utmost importance on the physical body, and takes worldly gains as the sole measure of life. Now, I often spend my days in pure joy like cooking while chanting *Dream*, watching robots sweep and mop the floor, and listening to Master's voice as it helps dissolve my habitual patterns. You know what? Marriage can actually be incredibly happy.

Our Master said, "You are both souls studying the Dharma. You both know to practice forgiveness, and you both know how to love yourselves and others. Therefore, such a family is bound to be happy."

Love is always about giving, not taking.

Depression

CAUSES OF DEPRESSION

There are three fundamental causes of depression. The first cause is the sense of not being understood. It's the feeling that "you don't understand what's on my mind. There's no one who can truly understand me, and I have no one to confide in." That is to say, within one's heart, the sense of loneliness, helplessness, confusion, and the bewilderment of losing oneself—those feelings cannot be expressed. When left unexpressed, these emotions accumulate over time, and form one's personality.

And because that personality is built on confusion, helplessness, loneliness, and bewilderment, it tends to see the world through a negative perspective. This is the first point: not being understood within the heart, and lacking an effective way to communicate. This is the first cause of depression.

The second cause is a lack of meaning: “My life has no meaning”—a sense of meaninglessness.

Depression isn’t something only poor people experience. Actually, it’s the opposite: poor people are less likely to suffer from it. Because they’re so busy just trying to survive, running around to make ends meet, they don’t have the energy or the spare time to be depressed. If he gets depressed today, there’s no food for today; if they get depressed tomorrow, he might starve to death. So, faced with the choice between starving to death and being depressed, I believe he’s definitely going to choose not to starve.

So, poor people are actually less likely to develop depression. Depression requires time—it needs time and space to take hold. Poor people rarely get depression. Those who do are generally the ones with money and leisure.

The third cause is a lack of love in the person’s heart.

It is not just the absence of feeling loved by others—more importantly, this person lacks the capacity to love others and the world. This point is crucial.

Depression arises under these three conditions: first, not being understood; second, lacking meaning; third, lacking love.

Cause 1: Not being understood

What does "not being understood" mean? For humans—what humans call understanding must be understanding the personality. I understand you, of what kind of person you are, what you like, and what you don't like. I understand what kind of confusion you have inside, what you plan to do, what goals you hope to achieve, how you intend to go about it, and how I can help you effectively in that process. When people talk about understanding, it is based on those personality-level needs. Let's say you're unhappy today—what's the reason? Right? You tell me the reason, only then can I help you.

This kind of understanding, in fact, barely addresses the fundamental psychological needs of people with depression. The reason people develop depression, and the reason they are not understood, is that the part of them longing to be understood lies in deep inner feelings, beyond the reach of personality, consciousness, and conventional moral values.

Even they themselves can't put it into words, because there's no clear reason for it, you know? There is no specific cause, no specific reason, no specific incident, and no specific manifestation. This is common ground for people with depression: that state where your heart is desperate to open up, to be truly understood, but you just can't find the words.

People refer to depression as a "cold of the soul." A cold may have a cause, but the actual experience of having a cold is very hard to describe in words. You might say, "I feel chills and fever, my whole body is shivering, I feel unwell."

But this "unwell" is only a concept. The discomfort one experiences is a feeling—and that feeling cannot be fully contained by the word "unwell."

Thus, the underlying tone and foundation of the depressed mind—an emotional sentiment so elusive it defies language—is often referred to as a "mental cold," a "psychological flu," or simply a "mental illness."

This illness is a real state, which is impossible—or very difficult—to solidify, abstract, distill, and articulate through concepts or subjective will. This is why people with depression are not understood.

But when he communicates normally with others, others think he seems perfectly fine. Why is that? Because normal communication must be built upon the continuity between mental motivation and consciousness. "Did you eat?" "Yes, I did." "There's work today, how did it go?" "I finished it." "How much did you get paid today?" "Six thousand five hundred." Okay, these are all concepts that mental cognition and conscious discrimination can reach—along with the psychological states of personality connected to those concepts. They can be described and expressed through language and consciousness.

But inside a person with depression, there exists another self hidden away in a dark corner. That hidden self is difficult to reach or describe using subjective motives and concepts of conscious distinction. They might suddenly, for no clear reason, sink into a feeling of being completely alone, like they're stranded on a deserted island, far from everyone else. You see him sitting, standing, laughing, and talking among others, yet inwardly he is cut off, isolated far away on that deserted island.

He may appear to be close to the crowd, standing just a few meters away, but his heart feels distant from this world, as if the world can never reach him, and he feels forever powerless to blend into the crowd. This is the kind of confusion arising from not being understood and not being able to put the state into words.

Depression is a truly terrifying "psychological illness." It extends beyond the scope of "mental illness"—it is a "psychological illness". When we speak of the psychological level, what we call "mental" refers to our consciousness and personality will—this is what we mean by "mental." Consciousness and personality include our subjective intentions, inner feelings, and emotional tendencies; all of these belong to the mental system.

Yet the mental system and our conscious thinking, residing at the surface of the psychological level, is the surface layer of our inner world. Beneath the surface layer, there are also the middle and even the deep layer of the inner world.

In someone with depression, the surface level of their inner world might look perfectly healthy, no different from anyone else's. Yet beneath the surface, the emotional factors that support personality intention and psychological needs have undergone alteration. This alteration directly prevents the person from integrating with society and from communicating with others.

What he is able to communicate is only the parts that can be shared within the realm of human life: my emotions, wishes, and motivations; my consciousness, thoughts, and concepts; my subjective consciousness will. These are things that can be communicated. But those deep, inner self-experiences that lie beyond subjective conscious will are difficult for his personality will to extract and articulate.

That is just like... Let me give you an example, so you can understand. Think of it like inflammation in the body caused by a virus or bacteria. But the way inflammation shows up can be so different: your gums might be inflamed, or your cornea, your lymph nodes might swell, you might get rheumatism in one joint, or have a painful, swollen spot somewhere else. There are countless forms of inflammation, with hundreds or even thousands of variations. But the root cause of inflammation is only one: your body's immune defenses have weakened.

Thus, the foundation—the underlying tone and the inner hue of the depressed mind reside in a diminished psychological immunity, fettered by those microscopic, negative sentiments that constitute the very fabric of personality and human nature.

This is the first point: not being understood, and moreover, having no way to make oneself understood. He is unable to express it, so how could others possibly understand? Because such understanding must transcend the realm of ordinary human life—only then can it penetrate the barriers of personality and human nature, perceive the fundamental, true state of elements that constitute personality and human nature, and then redeem him from the purgatory he is in.

Only when he is truly understood can he bring out the deep emotions within his heart.

If he confides in someone who does not understand him, such as his most trusted parents, and says, "I've felt recently that life has no meaning; I feel empty and bored; I have no interest in doing anything. I feel unable to integrate into the world, unable to fit in at school, and unable to share my inner state with my friends." What might his parents think? "It's just self-pity. You're just whining over nothing. You need a good spanking. Go without food for three days, and you'll be fine." If he talks to his friends, they might say, "You're just bored. Come on, let's grab a drink and some BBQ. That'll fix you right up. And if it doesn't, we'll do it again."

People can only address what you are able to express—you know? They have no way of resolving the inner experience formed by those deeply buried feelings that cannot be expressed.

In the first stage, the inner foundation of a depressed person is built on negative feelings and perceptions. Because those inner feelings are negative, the personality that grows from them becomes pessimistic and oppositional, sometimes even turning into a rejection of society itself.

This is the first key factor for a person with depression: not being understood. Moreover, the patient himself is unable to express the confusion within him, because those deep-

I will understand you.
I will take it on for you.

seated sentiments cannot be distilled by consciousness. Your conscious mind can put words to experiences like "I feel hurt. I'm in pain. I'm exhausted." It can extract experiences, but it can't capture the deeper feelings themselves. Do you see what I mean?

When I sense...inexplicably sense that the world has lost its appeal to me and I no longer have any interest in it, the consciousness can only register that this state is happening, but it cannot distill it into the question: "Why? What caused this?" Consciousness cannot reach the factors deep-seated within sentiments. Consciousness can only extract experiences, but it cannot extract the underlying reasons of sentiments deep within feelings of the heart.

Therefore, consciousness is unable to help with the state of "not being understood" or with the sense of isolation from the world experienced by people with depression. It cannot reach it, alleviate it, or comfort it. This is why, in later stages, people with depression often rely on medication. Psychological counselors are unable to help at this level.

Because human language must be an expression of consciousness and inner motivations—yet consciousness and these motivations cannot reach the deeper sentimental elements that underlie and constitute them.

So, counseling can help to a point, offering some temporary relief, but it can't get to the root cause. That's why, in the later stages, depression patients often have to take large amounts of medications—antidepressant medications, attempting to alter the chemical composition within the body in order to change their mental state. This approach causes significant damage to the body.

Cause 2: Life feels meaningless

What is the second state experienced by a person with depression? It is a sense of meaninglessness, a feeling that "my life has no meaning." This stems from the first state: the inability to be understood, and the inability to describe that state of not being understood. These give rise to a prolonged inner experience of isolation from the world, loneliness, and helplessness. When this inner state is projected onto one's personality and consciousness in the human world, it manifests as the view: "I myself have no meaning to live." It is not "no value," but "no meaning."

Do you understand what "having no meaning" really means? It means that no matter what I do, it's all pointless. Everything I do is non-essential. Whether I do good deeds or bad deeds, the world doesn't value me in the slightest. Everything I do and everything I am are like air in the eyes of the world. In other words, my very existence is meaningless, insignificant, overlooked by others, and forgotten by the world. In fact, this is a manifestation of the sense of loneliness due to not being understood, projected onto the human world through personality and consciousness.

But let me tell you something today. From the perspective of the ultimate Reality of life, the feeling of people with depression—that they are not understood and that their lives are completely worthless and meaningless—is "true". When they say "I feel that my life has no meaning," this statement is true. This is not just their subjective thought.

Because I am a practitioner. Practitioners are beings that straddle the realms of the Divine and the mortal. From the perspective of spiritual awakening, looking down at the human world, every person living in it has no inherent meaning. Because meaning by itself must be the value formed through comparison.

Do you see what I mean? Say I don't have a job and I just sit by the side of the road watching ants all day. People would say, "That person's life is completely meaningless." Why? Because meaning comes from comparing what you do to what others achieve.

You are not alone.
Love is with you.
We love you, praise you, and embrace you.

But if they knew I was a world-famous scientist who studies ants, then me spending my days "doing nothing" and crouching on the ground watching ants would be seen as in credibly meaningful. See? The whole idea of "meaning" comes from comparison. It is through comparison that so-called meaning and value are formed.

Yet the feeling of people with depression that their life has no meaning does not come from comparisons with others. Instead, it is a concrete manifestation, a tangible state of the negative life-sentiments within them, projected onto their personality, mind, and consciousness.

But in my opinion, this situation is correct. I believe it's right for people with depression to think that their lives have no value or meaning. Why? Because the soul of every life—each and every one, I'm talking about the ultimate Reality of every human life, is Heaven. That is the real meaning; that is the real value.

Because the true, original soul of a human being is infinite happiness, infinite light, infinite abundance, and endless joy. It is immutable and it never changes. It does not stand in opposition to the world, and thus is not distinguished by any relative matters. This is very difficult for humans to understand. It's like the clarity with which your eyes see the world—it doesn't change its nature of clarity just because the scenes you see in the world change.

Every soul on this earth has forgotten the eternal

wholeness and happiness of its innate Spirit of Life, and thus has become the present ego-personality. Your ego-personality, within its self-experience, has forgotten its innate, eternal, indestructible happiness, and the solemn, magnificent Light. People often feel startled and confused: Why have I come to this place? What is the meaning of my living? I suddenly feel that my existence in life has no meaning or value at all. This feeling is correct—it's just that no one has guided you on why it is correct.

From the worldly perspective, people would think you're "full and bored," doing something utterly pointless. But from my perspective, I believe this is your chance of awakening. Otherwise, Sakyamuni Buddha wouldn't have renounced the world to seek enlightenment.

There are typically two things about people with depression: First, their inner world is not understood by others; second, they feel that their lives are meaningless and lack value. These two conditions are exactly what give rise to the longing to witness one's own original nature—a weariness with the mundane world, renunciation of ordinary life, and a reverent pursuit of the Truth.

I believe that for people with depression, this psychological disorder can be an excellent opportunity for the soul's awakening—because you are truly not this body.

I find it truly a pity, you know—I think the passing of that female celebrity is such a great pity. I could have saved her. If she could—if only she could have waited a little longer, until someone delivered my recordings and books to her. If she had listened to them attentively, it probably wouldn't have taken long—only a few months. Then, her weak soul, trapped in a terminal illness, unable to extricate herself, only hiding in a dark corner quietly waiting for death, would have seen the light.

When the soul beholds the light of Heaven, she will awaken to the memories of the Life of Heaven. Once the memories of Heaven begin to revive, the self in the mundane world loses its value for existence.

In the beginning when you were suffering from depression, you thought that this self had no value. But when your true Life begins to awaken, you will realize that this worthless self truly has no value. Because the real "you" cannot be measured by value. He is infinite, eternal, radiant, and happy. He will never be altered by any arising, ceasing, coming or going thoughts and forms—He is immortal.

This is the fundamental reason why practitioners can transform the mindset of depression into the provisions for attaining enlightenment. In my view, for those in the human world, depression is an extremely rare opportunity for spiritual awakening. In other words, I believe that all souls living in the human world are in a state of death-like confusion and darkness—only they themselves are unaware of it.

I really don't know what meaning a human life has. Look, meaning is always relative. Suppose you could live for 100,000 years. With the current advanced technology on earth, everything you do during these 100,000 years would be valuable and meaningful. Every step you take would carry significance. Why? Because with a 100,000-year lifespan, you would still have over 99,900 years ahead of you. There's still so much time left, and there's a chance for a turnaround at any moment in the future. Your 100,000-year lifespan is long enough for you to accomplish many things. All the wealth, efforts, work, and educational background you have now become the capital for your 100,000-year life. You can expand infinitely, grow without limit, create countless different lives, and experience infinite variety of psychological, emotional, and physical states in these lives. This might barely qualify as having meaning.

A 100,000-year lifespan, although the pain you experience will always outweigh the happiness, still offers a sufficiently long expanse in which you can undergo both pain and happiness. But your lifespan—the human lifespan, only lasts a hundred years at most. For a lifespan of only around seventy, eighty, or ninety years, I really can't comprehend what meaning your so-called endeavors hold for your soul, as they will soon be swallowed by death, in the blink of an eye.

It's like a sandcastle a child builds on the beach. You can treat it as a toy. You spend four hours building it, and when the tide comes in, it will be washed away. It's okay to regard it as a game. It's for fun, right? Yet if you treat it as a permanent home, then you're in big trouble. If you want to build a castle on the beach to live in and bring your wife and children here, you're simply out of your mind.

You cannot build a house on sand. Therefore pursuing career success, family happiness, and a comfortable life in the human world is like building a sandcastle on the beach, as they are vanishing in the blink of an eye.

The lifespan of a sandcastle might be just four hours, while your human life lasts only seventy or eighty years, which also passes in the blink of an eye. However, your soul will never die. When the sandcastle is destroyed, the child who built it can go home, find his mother, wash up, and go to sleep. But what about you? After the sandcastle—which you've built over these seventy or eighty years in the human world—is submerged by the sea of death, where can you go?

Therefore, I believe that when those suffering from depression feel that there is no value, no meaning in the human world, they are not wrong—because this is the very Suchness of life. However, they're just missing one thing. They don't know what is real. They only know that everything in their current life is false, but they have no idea what is truly real. In other words, when the seawater destroys the sandcastle on the beach, if the child doesn't know where his home is, then he'll be in a very miserable situation.

When death comes and takes away your body, wealth, emotions, and appearance in this lifetime, along with your happiness and all your self-related experiences, where will your soul go? This is something you don't know, and that's why you'll fall into a state of panic.

The second state of people with depression is the feeling that life is meaningless. That's because they don't know what the real meaning is. The real meaning for life lies in returning to Heaven. Because Heaven is more real than the human world, which is constantly changing in every moment.

Your body is constantly moving toward death without a pause. In eighty or ninety years, you'll just be a pile of dry bones on the ground, or perhaps a handful of ashes in a crematorium. Your current house, car, wife, children, lovers, and bank savings have absolutely nothing to do with that pile of ashes. Therefore, all the things you have now have nothing to do with you either, because you're destined to end up as that pile of ashes.

I've told you that there's no value or meaning in the human world, but no one has ever told you where its true value lies. The value of the human world lies in this: while you still have a body, consciousness, and the capacity for inner experience, you can hear the Truth and awaken, within your life—the Spirit Heaven that has been veiled for countless ages by your ego-consciousness and mental cognition. That is the eternal, indestructible, truly real, immutable, and forever joyful Reality of life. This is the value and meaning that every soul in the human world should awaken to, which is to return to Heaven. While you are alive, awaken the Life of Heaven within your body and mind—that is the only meaning of your life.

When Heaven awakens within your life, those inner, negative emotions and deep-seated self-experiences within your heart—the ones that are hard to describe, hard to bring up, hard to articulate, and difficult to comprehend—will vanish without a trace. Because they are all karmic accumulations carried through life; they are memories of darkness formed in life through cycles of birth and death. These have obscured your soul's memory of the radiant Heaven. When the light is gone, only darkness remains. And when darkness becomes you, your depression becomes incurable.

Conversely, when the light of Heaven shines through your mind-consciousness and into your inner experiences, deep within your inner experience, those memories of darkness that form the very fabric of experience will be dispelled by the radiant light of Heaven. When the light of Heaven dissipates the dark memories in sentiments and life, your depression will vanish instantly.

My teaching method has a 100% success rate in healing depression, but it requires time. Some people may recover in as little as two or three months. Those who have suffered from depression for many years, or even more than a decade, may need several years, one to four years, for instance, to recover fully.

However, there is one prerequisite for my method of treating depression: you must believe in the existence of Deity. If you're an atheist, I cannot save you. You must meet a prerequisite: you need to adopt a different perspective to view life. You can't view life through the lens of current human science and technology. Rather, you need to perceive life from the perspective of an Enlightened One and through rational and dialectical thinking.

In my heart, in my eyes, and in my wisdom, life is immortal. Because in fact, you are not truly alive right now. The body you have now—your current body is false; it is not truly alive.

Our bodies are composed of cells. Beneath the cells, there are proteins, nucleic acids, and DNA. Going further down, there are molecules, atoms, and the exploration can even reach quarks. In the realm of science, there is currently no way to prove the existence of quarks... No existing scientific technology is capable of detecting these quark particles. Scientists have only inferred, based on the observed behavior of matter, that there exists a fundamental form of energy at the microscopic level of the universe, which they call quarks.

A quark is born and extinguished once every one five-hundred-thousandth of a second, meaning that within just one second, it goes through the cycle of birth and death five hundred thousand times. Within a single second, it is born and dies five hundred thousand times. In other words, our bodies, minds, sensations, inner experiences, cognition of ego-personality, and our consciousness and memories undergo five hundred thousand times of birth and death within just a single second.

It is through the extremely rapid, continuous cycles of birth and death—five hundred thousand births and deaths per second—that the functioning of our cells, the workings of our thoughts, the experience of our emotions, and the continuity of our sensations are manifested. Do you understand? You and I are nothing but appearances in the human world, arising from the causes and conditions in the continuous moment-to-moment births and deaths. It's like a person made of sand—if you look closely at the micro level, there is not any human figure inside the sand. The sand merely forms the appearance of a person. But when you examine it at a microscopic level, the so-called human form doesn't exist at all.

So, for people with depression, your perception of the world should be from the perspective of Buddhism. Do not view it through the conventional concepts you've acquired in the mundane world, such as the idea that a person is born from parents, that a fertilized egg develops into a fetus, then is born, grows up, and eventually dies. Do not perceive it in this way.

A basic condition for changing a person with depression is to transform their outlook on life, and help them learn to view life from a wise perspective. This is because a person's inner experiences follow cognition. Just like the clouds in the sky, which drift wherever the wind takes them.

When a person is extremely thirsty and wants water, you hand them a glass of water and tell them, "There's potassium cyanide in it. Drinking it will surely kill you." Even though they're very thirsty, they wouldn't dare to drink it, you know? This shows that cognition determines experience. If you tell them, "Although this glass of water looks murky, it's full of nutrients and tastes great," even though the water looks unpalatable, they'll still drink it. This is what we mean by cognition determining experience.

Cause 3: Lack of love

The third cause is a lack of love, meaning that people with depression lack the ability in their heart to love themselves and the world. In reality, being loved by others—for an individual life—brings only a very small, limited experience of being loved.

Because between loving and being loved, there is a giver and a recipient, right? The one who receives love, in fact, doesn't truly experience love deeply.

Because love must be an expression, you know? Love is always manifested. When I say "I love you," or "you are my life," when I hold you in my arms every day, kiss you, bring you delicious food, or even go without nice clothes or good drinks myself so I can give them to you, when I give you my most cherished possessions, I express my love through these actions.

Love must be expressed in some way, right? Whenever

love is expressed through words, forms or actions, the purity of love is already greatly diminished. However, for the person giving love, the experience of love is incredibly intense and feels almost absolute. Because the giving of love by the one who gives love...Bear in mind, bear in mind—what is the core of love? The core of love is selflessness; anything selfish cannot be called love—that is merely an exchange, an emotional exchange.

I saw a very beautiful woman. I was fixated on the idea of sleeping with her, so I bought her many gifts and sent her flowers every day. My intention was to sleep with her. Can you call this kind of behavior love? That is desire.

On the contrary, when it comes to your own child, the one who came straight out of your womb, everything you do for him is absolutely without asking for return. There's absolutely no way you'd ask for anything in return. Suppose him kicks off the blanket in the middle of the night. No matter how tired you are, even with your eyes closed, you will instinctively fumble for a blanket to cover him. It's all subconscious, instinctive. That is love. You see?

The core of love must be selflessness; the core of love must be free from any expectation. To give selflessly without expecting any return—that is love. Precisely because it is such pure giving, free from any expectation or selfishness, the experience of love for the one who gives is profoundly deep and intense.

Love itself cannot be extracted either. Just as the loneliness and darkness within a depression patient cannot be understood or distilled, the true power of love also cannot be extracted through consciousness and language. In other words, only love has the power to withstand the negative sentiments within the hearts of those suffering from depression. Because they exist in the same realm of inner world—a dimension that consciousness and mind cannot reach, refine, or transform.

Only love can truly redeem, transform, and heal the lonely, dark, negative feelings in the hearts of those suffering from depression—the sense of isolation, of not being understood, of alienation, and of meaninglessness. Only love can.

So, how does this kind of love manifest in the human world? There are two ways. The first is by being needed by others.

When a person experiences increasing love and affirmation from others, they grow more confident. When someone feels others' forgiveness, acceptance, and warmth in their inner experience, they become more secure.

Let me tell you, I rarely hear of mothers with young children committing suicide. Yes, there are such cases, but they are very rare. Why? Because the child needs you. Because the child you are holding needs you to raise. When his tender little hands clutch yours and he looks up at you calling you "Mommy," you bear a responsibility.

Even if a mother had to pick up trash for a living, or to put it bluntly, even if she became a sex worker to provide for her child, I see nothing shameful in her actions. I truly don't. Maybe my outlook on life and my moral values are different from others'. I value authenticity, and I particularly despise those self-righteous moral preachers.

During World War II, there was a true story. I think it was when the German troops either occupied Poland or the Soviet Union. They captured a young mother whose baby might have been only a few months old. To protect her child from being harmed by those German soldiers, the mother endured being raped by more than twenty of them without putting up any resistance. Eventually, it seems that because of this, the mother survived. Although those German soldiers were brutal beasts, they spared the lives of both the mother and her child.

If this had happened in ancient China, it would have been the end for her—her chastity ruined, she would've been condemned to die without a proper burial. I believe that kind of thinking—that mindset is truly worse than being a beast. You know what I mean? It shows a complete disrespect for basic humanity—that so-called doctrine of "preserving heavenly principle and extinguishing human desire." But did they not realize? The man who preached it was committing adultery with his daughter-in-law, and even got two nuns pregnant. Don't you think that's utterly ridiculous?

As living beings in this world, it's only right that we abide by laws and regulations. But even more so, we should respect the fundamental aspects of human nature and human dignity. Don't let so-called moral concepts destroy the most fundamental conscience and integrity that come with being human.

That mother was willing to be violated by those beasts in order to save her child from being killed. Everything she did to protect the life of her own child—I think that mother is truly remarkable, you know? I believe that mother is incredibly great! Absolutely amazing—that's what a mother truly is!

I don't believe that a mother like that—one who could endure such inhumane humiliation for the sake of her child—would ever suffer from depression. No way. Why? Because the love in her heart outweighs her instinct to protect herself. A person who loves others more than they love themselves could never suffer from depression—it's simply impossible.

Remember, what I say is the Truth. A person who loves others more than he loves himself will never cross paths with depression in this lifetime. Depression will never come knocking on his door, because love is the nemesis of depression—just as light is the nemesis of darkness.

If a person with depression does not encounter the Truth, and relies solely on worldly moral codes and medical treatments to heal, then at best it can only bring temporary relief—it cannot cure the root of the problem. But if he can listen to the Dharma, study the Dharma, and personally experience within his heart what true love, selfless love is—then his depression can be cured without medicine.

I have never believed that a person who has love in their heart—who loves others, loves society, loves other people more than themselves—could ever suffer from depression. It's absolutely impossible. Not even a 0.001% chance. No possibility whatsoever. All those who suffer from depression do so because they have lost the ability to love in their hearts.

HOW TO HEAL DEPRESSION

Then there are two solutions. The first is to find a way to feel needed and valued by others. Even rescuing a stray cat or dog counts. I'm talking about rescuing, not adopting. Adopting, I imagine, might be beyond your means, as the cost of caring for a pet can be quite substantial.

Since you don't even want to live anymore, right? Then take out some of your daily living expenses. For example, if you usually spend thirty or fifty yuan on meals every day, set aside forty yuan to buy some cat or dog food and take it to feed those stray cats and dogs. You're someone on the verge of giving up on life. What are you afraid of? Since you don't even want to live, why can't you spare some of your money to help other animals live a better life? Huh? Don't you have this bit of generosity? You're on the brink of death—you don't want to live anymore. What do you need so much money for? Use it to save other lives and add a little bit of light to your otherwise humble existence. Being needed by others is one of the ways

to help those with depression.

The second approach is to pray for the Divine's blessing. Why do the vast majority of scientists and accomplished people in society tend to embrace religion in their later years—especially after the age of 60? Because of their rich experiences and accumulated wisdom in the world, after decades of reflection and personal insight, and through observation and contemplation, they have come to realize that many things in life simply cannot be achieved by human effort alone. That is called a miracle. Through their own experiences, and through comparison and reflection in the long span of life, they come to know that fate exists—and where there is fate, there must be someone who arranges it. Thus they choose to believe in God or in the Buddha.

When a person's heart gives rise to faith in the Divine—the real Divine, the True Divine—then that Spirit Heaven within you, which has been veiled for hundreds of thousands of millions of kalpas by your personality and the ego of mental cognition, will awaken from the depths of your life, with a feeling of déjà vu, as though across lifetimes—because Heaven is the Divine's own body.

When your mind has faith in the Divine, a profound sense of peace, purity, excitement, and joy will awaken spontaneously within every cell of your being, throughout your consciousness and emotions, in a way that feels beyond your control.

When the light of Heaven inherent in your life awakens from within the cells of your body, your consciousness, and memories of your heart, those sentiments of the depressive self and dark memories of life will automatically dissipate. This is the second method: faith in the Divine can dispel depression.

The Divine is truly real—more real than human existence,

far more real—because the Divine is unchanging. He never changes, He is eternal, and He is whole. There is no separation between the world and me in Him; rather, all worlds and all life exist within Him. His wholeness and light are never fractured by the mental distinctions of the world and sentient beings. It is only that beings are veiled by their own minds and consciousness, which obscure the light of Heaven innate within life—and thus they become the self lost in confusion and depression. Yet your true nature is none other than eternal, boundless love and light. That is Heaven.

Guide those who suffer from depression to have faith in Heaven. Let them know that Heaven is more real than the human world, and that the Divine is more real than humankind. Help them awaken to the realm of heavenly light, eternity, and happiness that has always been within their life—in this way depression can also heal.

Depression stems from dark memories buried deep in the mind, which form a barrier that blocks access to the memory of light in one's mind and consciousness.

When this state is projected onto the personality, it manifests as weariness, a sense of meaninglessness, loss of love, and even loss of the will to live.

In the later stages, depression patients may even find breathing difficult. I have experienced this firsthand. It's not that I have depression myself, but that I've delved deep into the minds of those who suffer from depression. Every breath they take is as difficult as carrying a sack weighing hundreds of pounds. Why is that? There is no longer any light within them to support the soul, thus the soul is dragged by the subtle habits and delusions accumulated over countless lifetimes into a dark predicament. Every single moment of their existence is sheer torment and suffering.

I'm telling you the truth. You don't understand the pain that depression patients go through, but I do. They truly endure extreme agony every single minute and every single second of their lives. It's a kind of despair and anguish in the heart. Even taking each breath is an extremely difficult and painful experience. That's why they choose to end their lives, in an attempt to put an end to this endless and hopeless suffering.

That's because they've forgotten the complete and luminous Heaven within their own lives, and thus have been drawn into this abyss of despair and helplessness by the dark memories of life. So, what we need to do is to reveal the light of Heaven to them, allowing their souls to perceive the true nature of their lives via their consciousness and personality. Once their lives develop a longing for the Truth, their Spirit awakens within the Truth, and the innate light of Heaven in their lives naturally shines forth, all the dark memories will be instantly eradicated, and they will become whole and healthy individuals.

For someone suffering from depression—no matter how long you have been trapped in it, how hopeless the situation has become, how painful your condition feels, or how agonizing your inner experience is—believe me, believe me: as long as you listen to my recorded teachings, and as long as you persist and listen through to the end, your soul will be made new. For I will send your soul to Heaven, and you will surely recover.

Cases

COLLEGE STUDENT CONFRONTS THE BIPOLAR ABYSS (PART 1)

Let me share a few thoughts on psychological illness: Be truly authentic—honestly face your inner self, sincerely express your feelings to your family, and wholeheartedly open yourself to the Divine.

The other night, just before going to bed, I watched a short recap of the third episode of the American series Modern Love. Starring the gorgeous Anne Hathaway, the episode portrays a woman with bipolar disorder who yearns deeply for love and to be loved. However, her illness caused her moods to swing wildly; at times she felt euphoric and full of engergy, while at other times she became so depressed and hopeless that she could not even leave her house and instead curled up in bed. As a result, the small spark of love was painfully extinguished just as it began to kindle.

For years, she never disclosed her illness and the pain she

endured to the people around her. At the very end of the episode, she finally confided in her female boss, poured out her heart, and reached out to her relatives and friends to explain her past withdrawal and the hurt she had caused them. In that moment of genuine vulnerability, she was met with understanding.

Apart from serious physical illnesses, I also suffer from bipolar disorder, also known as manic depression. When I'm in a good state, I feel bright and full of charm. When I'm in a manic episode, I become irrational and unable to think clearly. When I'm depressed, I spiral into self-blame, self-pity, and even self-harm.

I understand people with depression, bipolar disorder, and anxiety who wear a smiling mask in public. Many may seem cheerful and upbeat on the outside, but when they're alone, their inner world feels empty and cold. They're afraid to face the dark void within because it feels like a place that could suddenly unleash terrifying monsters, ready to devour their souls at any moment.

But the most crucial reason is that they simply don't know

how to face it and lack the strength to do so. This isn't just the pain of a single lifetime, nor is it the so-called family-of-orgin trauma that psychologists often speak of. Instead, it is the pain of the soul accumulated over countless lifetimes, a tremendous sense of fear and insecurity that seems to come out of nowhere.

When one is powerless to face their inner turmoil, withdrawal and confrontation become instinctive responses. Withdrawal allows the darkness to grow ever stronger, while confrontation turns this non-existent darkness into a tangible reality, trapping one in an inescapable cycle of suffering.

They do not realize that there is another path in this world, one that involves facing reality with honesty, embracing love, and turning the heart toward the Truth.

Often, when we're in pain, we're reluctant to show our true selves to others. We put on disguises, offer perfunctory responses, hide away, or slam the door and storm off.

"I'm fine. I'm good. I'm not angry at all. I'm not sad at all. I'm very easy-going..." In fact, we may be on the verge of exploding inside. I used to have this problem myself. But since last year, I've been making continuous efforts to change myself and trying my best to face my true self.

For example, I have a strong sense of jealousy. But the worst thing isn't having jealousy itself. It's being jealous yet being too afraid to face it, automatically rationalizing and justifying that jealousy in my mind, concealing it, and staying away from situations that trigger the feeling.

Later, I chose to face it head-on. I used to be tormented by jealousy, trapped in it and suffering deeply. But now, I can immediately become aware of it. Once I notice it, I allow it to flow through me. The moment I see it, I speak it out, embrace and forgive it.

I chose to face the venomous serpent in my heart. Time and again, I let go of everything, closed my eyes, and opened my arms wide. I allowed it to pounce on me, to bite me, even to tear me to pieces. Yet I simply held it gently in a warm embrace. Gradually, within my open heart, its power grew ever weaker.

I am not emotional pain. I am love, forgiveness, and acceptance.

Another powerful emotion is anger. There are times when I'm fine one moment, and the next, I'm knocked to the ground by a huge, surging wave of anger. Before I developed this condition, I wasn't like this. I used to be simple, honest, generous, emotionally stable, and full of warmth.

But what should I do now? This is my karma, my fate. It has already come. I'm no longer my former self. At this very moment, I'm no angel; I'm a devil.

Can you imagine a pretty little girl who suddenly has an emotional outburst the next second, sitting at the mall entrance, crying her eyes out, convulsing all over, and glaring fiercely at anyone she sees? When you meet such a person, all you can do is shout "crazy person!" and run away as fast as you can.

I tell myself that I'm just listening attentively. Anger is like a constantly crying child, and I am the mother of this child, not its enemy. I need to listen to the child's pain and grievances with all my attention. I'll embrace it with a soft heart and take care of it. The moment I smile, I've already distanced myself from it.

I'll tell myself that I give full permission. I allow anger to run wild, as if I've turned into a huge fishing net with countless holes, letting the seawater flow through instead of blocking it.

Gradually, after a few minutes, the pressure begins to ease, and the anger starts to subside. Finally, I silently repeat "I forgive you, I bless you, I love you", open my arms, embrace it, and let it melt into love.

However, the foundation for facing up to things and extending love is devout faith in the Divine. I'm just a frail human being. How could I have the strength to contend with the karmic creditors from countless past lives? Only through devout faith, only through detachment, only through learning my Master's Teachings, and only through trusting in the Truth. Once again, I'm reminded of that passage in the teaching *Compassion*:

"Therefore, for a true practitioner, if you follow my path,

which is the path of attainment through forgiveness, it means integrating the love of the Truth and complete forgiveness into your daily life. Forgive your own fears. Embrace your own habitual tendencies. Through loving acceptance and compassion, understand your own vices, pettiness, resistance, greed, jealousy, hatred, and cruelty. Learn to understand the pettiness within your heart, and to understand the coldness and pain that dwell within you. With the pure and warm love of the Truth, embrace yourself, forgive yourself, warm yourself, accept yourself, understand yourself, and hold yourself with compassion. Until your heart becomes warm and melts into the infinite, boundless, and endless pure light of the Truth's love—into its eternal warmth and acceptance—you will naturally be able to extend this warmth of acceptance to everyone around you. This is called redemption by compassion. Over time, your inner spiritual awareness will manifest through the peace and warm love in your heart. When the mind within you is embraced, warmed, and forgiven by the love of the Truth, the fear and habitual patterns within your mind will gradually dissolve."

Now, when I'm in pain, I try my best to tell my family, "I'm in great pain. I feel so angry. But I'm trying my best. I'm becoming aware of and embracing my emotions. Please give me a hug, stroke my hand, and let me have some quiet time alone."

When images from the past flash through my mind and I recall those who have hurt me, if I feel wronged, I allow myself to cry naturally. I might even shout, "I hate you all. I despise you!"

But at the same time, I'm aware of my own crying and complaining. I know this isn't just a simple vent. Then, I allow my feelings of hatred to flow freely, embrace them, and forgive them.

The external enemies and the hatred within me are one and the same. As my feelings of hatred gradually fade away, my perception of that person also fades. Perhaps it will come back again next time. Well, then I'll be ready to face it head-on. Anyway, I have my ways, don't I?

In daily life, I often remind myself of this mantra:
"I am loved. I am deeply loved."

Cases

College student confronts the bipolar abyss (Part 2)

I've been reading the teachings for a little over a month, and the results are astonishing—whether in the purification of the body, mind, and cells; the large-scale dismantling of habits and desires; or the transformation of the lower-realm experiences my soul once harbored.

Recently, I've been reading out the teachings loudly every morning and evening. Aside from the changes in myself, it has also subtly influenced my family, giving them a lot of confidence.

Seeing the positive changes in me, my mom also began practicing the teachings. During our breaks, we exchange our thoughts with each other. Since the release of the lecture *Heaven of the Mind*, I have started regularly opening up to her by confessing, sharing my real thoughts, and catching my ego before it takes over. This open sharing and self-disclosure have helped us better integrate spiritual practice into daily life.

I've been suffering from an illness that caused my muscles to atrophy for over a decade. But after just over a month of reading the teachings, I've actually grown new muscle. You can see the new muscle definition when I roll up my sleeves or pants, and the new muscle feels firm and strong when you touch it.

I hadn't been able to eat much for many years. Even a small amount of food would cause severe stomach pain. But after reading the teachings for just over a month, I'm suddenly able to eat a lot. I can often wolf down a big meat bun.

Although such changes are surface-level, the key does not lie in clinging to them. What matters is cultivating gratitude and appreciation for Heaven at the same time. In that gratitude and longing for Heaven, Heaven is with us.

Our Master is incredibly compassionate. He treats us as gently as one would soothe a little, little child.

"It's okay when you say, 'I ate a steamed bun yesterday, and it tasted really good. This is blessing I've gained since I started practicing the teachings. In the past, I had no sense of taste, but now, after learning the teachings, I can enjoy the bun.' You ate a steamed bun and thought it was delicious. It's okay that this thought has led you to feel grateful and trusting toward the teachings. This trust is the opportunity for me to save you and take you to Heaven."

"As long as you have even a single thought of the Divine, whether it is accidental or fleeting, like 'Wow, Master's teachings sound really comforting. I've been sleeping better these past couple of days', that very thought is an olive branch extended to you by Heaven. Follow that thought, and your soul will return to that blissful holy realm: one of eternal warmth, eternal light, where there is never darkness, never death, and never suffering."

"As long as you have even the slightest bit of faith in the Truth, that is the start of me saving your soul. Heaven is only redemption and love, with no punishment." —Teaching: "The Tathagata (Part II)" (July 26, 2023)

After practicing the teachings, large chunks of deep-rooted

habits have disappeared. Previously, I tried to get rid of my ingrained flaws and habits through willpower, self-control, and self-discipline, but in the process of practicing the teachings, these problems just effortlessly disappeared.

For example, I used to love overspending and going shopping. My heart was always in a state of dissatisfaction, hoping to fill this inner void with external things. But during the practice of the teachings, this habit was quickly purified. It wasn't the result of my own efforts to restrain myself. Without any force, it just happened naturally. The feelings of depression, oppression, suffocation, and dissatisfaction that often arose in my heart disappeared.

Also, during my previous manic episodes—which were extremely torturous experiences—my heart would be in turmoil, overflowing with uncontrollable hatred, anger, cruelty, and impulses toward self-harm, along with a victim mentality.

These indescribable, deep-seated dark elements have also dissolved and been purified to a great extent.

In the past, those were hopeless, freezing cold nights. I had to face my inner emotions alone, writhing in agony, screaming and crying bitterly time and time again. I even lost control and lashed out at my loved ones with harsh words. Now, amazingly, I've gotten through those difficult times so effortlessly under my Master's guidance. I can hardly believe it.

Over the past month or so since I started practicing the teachings, I've lost my temper a few times. But my mom said it was just like a child throwing a tantrum, where they sulk and act up for a few minutes before it passes. Once it's over, I forget all about it. There's nothing left—no lingering emotions, no inner tension, nothing.

A heartfelt gratitude to our Master, for opening this rocket-like pathway of practicing the teachings. It has enabled sentient beings like me, burdened with heavy karmic obstacles, to receive such rapid salvation!

Behind the profound teachings lie countless gods and Buddhas!

Aside from physical illnesses, I also suffer from mental disorders. In 2019, I was hospitalized. There was a young fellow patient in the adjacent ward who had the same severe bipolar disorder as me. We underwent the same treatment and took the same medications. Her physical condition was quite good, with no issues at all. In contrast, my body was on the verge by collapse, and I endured a great deal of pain every day.

The night my parents rushed me to the emergency room, the doctor conducted a thorough examination and assessed my condition. My organs were already failing, and the doctor, with a grave expression, said I had only 7 to 10 days to live.

However, with my Master's guidance and redemption, I gradually recovered. Yet the girl who was nearly ten years younger than me and should have been enjoying a life as vibrant as spring flowers, tragically ended her own life at the end of this April due to unbearable pain.

I can do nothing on my own, and there's no way I can save myself. Only the Divine can save the souls of humanity.

I've been studying the teachings every day, and although it hasn't been very long, the wisdom, light, and love have been deeply cleansing, bringing a sense of renewal to both my mind and body.

After undergoing electroconvulsive therapy (ECT) eight times, most people would often become “like a fool.” From reading many accounts, I found that people often couldn’t remember anything and their work and studies suffered. This, in turn, led to further stress, depression, and anxiety.

But I’m getting better year by year. Although my memory hasn’t fully recovered to the level it was before I got sick, my ability to learn is gradually coming back. Now, even the more complex and profound things in my studies don’t seem difficult to understand.

I used to think winter was incredibly hard to endure, but I don’t feel that way anymore. The other day, I came across a quote by Camus: “In the depths of winter, I finally learned that within me there lay an invincible summer.” That summer is my Master, the Truth, the Divine.

“Only the Divine can save people. Humans in the teachings have no power to save themselves, nor do they have the power to save others.”

“Therefore, an absolute, sincere love for the Truth can help you, when you are trapped in the endless abyss of despair and pain, draw on the power of that love. It enables you to see the suffering self within and find redemption.” —Teaching: “Deliverance” (September 26, 2023)

Filmed on December 7, 2023

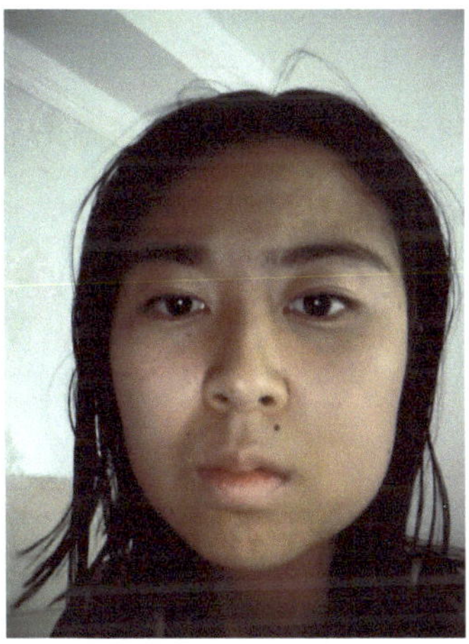

Filmed on July 24, 2019

Cases

Once severely depressed, I saw the light again

In 2018, I was struck by an episode of severe clinical depression. I quit my job and shut myself away at home, never venturing outside. I was terrified of seeing people or even sunlight. My days and nights were completely reversed, and I lived in a constant state of darkness. I obsessively played video games to escape from reality, refusing to communicate with anyone while isolating myself. My mind was consumed by thoughts of ending my life in various ways. I had lost all hope for the future; my spirit withered away, and my mind grew numb and listless. I became resentful, full of anger, and my face reflected the darkness within. I lost so much weight that I became gaunt like a skeleton. All that remained inside me was despair, torment, loneliness, and the relentless thought of suicide.

At the end of July 2019, I completely gave up everything and embarked on the path of studying the teachings.

Deep down in my heart, I was lost and helpless. My personality was fragile and incompetent, and my mind was filled with murderous thoughts. The thought of "kill, kill, kill" kept popping up. I wanted to escape from reality and run away, but I had nowhere to go.

No matter how painful it was copying the teachings, I persevered. Most of the time, I was carried away by my old habits. I often felt exhausted and slept a lot. A simple idea began to form: as long as I was awake, I would copy the teachings. My muddled heart was still swept away by dark and negative emotions every single second, and I was in a dull, stiff, and numb state.

In 2020, deep down in my heart, I was still consumed by fear and agony. My heart was as cold and hard as ice. I forced myself to keep studying. Though I was unwilling to give up or walk away, I approached the study in a lax and inconsistent manner, like fishing for three days and drying the net for two. Meanwhile, karmic retribution struck back relentlessly.

In 2021, I was still plagued by fear, anxiety, and restlessness.

I had an audio loop of *Dream* and *Peace of Mind* playing beside my bed 24 hours a day. As I attempted to resume communication with others, the inner barriers that had kept me closed off began to weaken, and my heart underwent a preliminary transformation. I continued to study the teachings.

The year 2022 marked the beginning of a turning point in my life. My spiritual practice moved through cycles of ebb and flow, bringing long-buried negative emotions to the surface. I was forced to confront a series of painful decisions. As my body and mind began to renew themselves, I struggled to let go.

Since the start of 2023, my spiritual practice has entered a phase of rapid advancement and purification. For most of the first half of the year, I lingered in a state of depression. Deep-seated sorrow lingered, negative emotions surged, and fear refused to loosen its grip.

From the second half of 2023 onward, I wore earphones 24 hours a day to listen to the latest audio teachings, and devoted myself to extensive scripture copying and reading. My inner state entered a completely new phase:

Only when living within the teachings can I be my true self. Deep in my heart, there is now warmth and love that nourish me. The fear and anxiety are gradually diluting and fading away. I no longer resist communication, nor do I feel defensive or averse toward the people I meet. My heart has turned inward toward itself, and I've become much simpler as a person. Whenever I didn't study the teachings, I felt as if something were missing—my heartfelt empty, helpless, and lost. After copying and reading the teachings, I felt energized and uplifted—bright and optimistic, light in both body and mind, and inwardly at peace. My soul seemed bathed in holy light, redeemed again and again, and continually reborn.

I still experience fear and unease, but I'm no longer afraid. The force of karmic backlash striking my heart is steadily weakening, and the tearing, tug-of-war within my inner being is gradually dissolving. I firmly believe that for a soul that passionately loves the Truth and yearns for Heaven, depression has long since faded away.

I'm breathing with a sense of solid grounding and relief, as if I've cast off a heavy burden.

Just like the poem goes, "The light boat has sailed past the ten thousand mountains!"

Our lives were saved by our beloved Master. Our Master watches over our souls, right in the depths of our being!

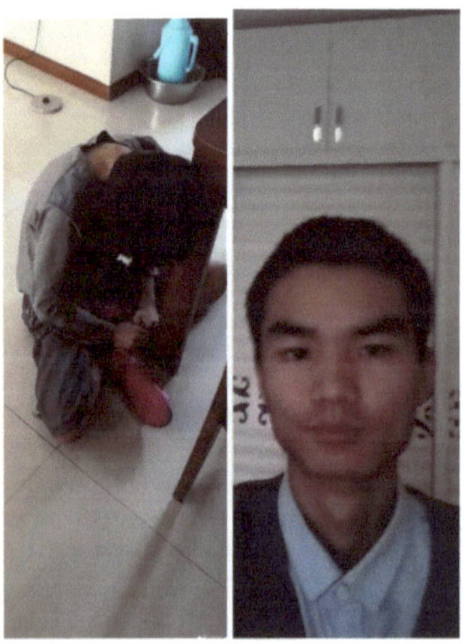

Filmed in 2018

Filmed in 2023

Cases

AFTER A LONG SEARCH, I FINALLY FOUND THE PATH TO RECOVERY

These days, I've been listening to my Master's recording—*Depression*. Reflecting on my past, I'm writing down my inner journey.

Our family did not have a very healthy emotional atmosphere. Before my parents turned ten, my grandmother and my maternal grandfather both died by suicide. By the time I was in junior high school, around the age of twelve or thirteen—an age when children are typically carefree and lively—I was the complete opposite. I wasn't as lively and outgoing as other kids. I often thought that death would be a better option and that life was meaningless.

Even after I got married and had children, my relationship with my spouse remained strained. We argued constantly, and our home felt perpetually gloomy. Fortunately, I had my son. The moment I saw him, my mood lifted, and all my worries faded away.

In recent years, as my son grew up and I had more time to myself, the signs of depression became increasingly obvious. What was that state like? Thoughts of "just go die" kept popping up in my mind, and scenes of hanging myself would constantly emerge. I felt like I was sinking all the way down. There was always a heavy lid pressing on my chest, making it hard to breathe. I found everything meaningless and had no interest in anything. I just wanted to die, so badly!

Did I lack love? Actually, no—I was deeply loved by my parents from childhood. But I didn't know how to love others. Apart from loving my child, I had become a resentful, bitter person. With the tension in my marriage, I was always looking for someone to complain to. That was the state I used to be in.

Later, I really couldn't hold on any longer and went to a therapist. However, I'm not good at expressing myself. The counselor said I wasn't articulate, and I felt hurt again. I went there a few times and then stopped going.

Later, I joined an online class. The instructor, who

claimed to be a psychologist specializing in Zen and Esoteric Buddhism, helped me achieve some improvement. I spent over 100,000 yuan in a little over a year, which amounted to my entire two-year salary! The instructor kept saying "guard your thoughts well". Guard your thoughts and change your perception. However, I still had doubts in my heart. What standards should we follow to change our perception? I also wanted to change my perception. I also wanted to guard my thoughts well. But my thoughts were beyond my control. They popped up anytime and anywhere!

I was lost in confusion again.

That's when I came across *Dream*. I transcribed *Dream* for half a month, and then I felt as if a heavy burden had been lifted from my heart. Every day, I was full of energy. Those frequent thoughts of wanting to die rarely bothered me anymore. The stuffy feeling in my heart was like a lid being lifted, and I could breathe in fresh air. I could even sense hope!

I've come to realize that my ego-personality is inherently unreal. Driven by this inherently illusory personality, I've been drifting between highs and lows, swinging between joy and

When one fully devotes the inner being and spiritual longing to the Truth, he can fundamentally heal the darkness within the mind, thus, depression will no longer exist.

sorrow, and getting deeply immersed in the illusions of life.

Now that I have a clear direction in life, a spiritual home for my soul, and a purpose to strive for, my only concern is not moving too slowly or falling behind on the way home. So, I no longer have the time or inclination to be depressed. All I think about now is how to remove the impurities from my heart, in accordance with the Truth. It is my Master who has given me a new lease on life and made me realize that we don't live just for the sake of living; we live to return home!

Having tried conventional psychological counseling methods, as well as those that blend Zen with mainstream psychology, a former depression sufferer has come to deeply realize that only here, with this Master, can one truly be reborn and have the roots of depression cut off. Our true Life exists in a place beyond the reach of body, speech, and mind. The "I" we perceive is not the real Self. Bathed in the light of the Truth, let love melt away the cold, dark corners within us. Those suffering from depression, come home. This is our shared warm and loving home!

Cases

ONCE, MY WORLD CAME CRASHING DOWN

Back when "depression" wasn't even recognized as an illness, and long before it became as prevalent as it is today, I was already battling with depression. I've been depressed since childhood.

During my childhood, my depression mainly manifested as fear, anxiety, and terror. I was constantly scared of making careless mistakes and angering my mother, or of getting poor grades and being scolded or beaten when I got home. As a result, I lived my life walking on eggshells, in constant fear. Whenever my mother was at home, I was the most obedient little girl imaginable. But when she was out, I'd turn into my father's precious little princess and finally have the chance to laugh happily, although such opportunities were few and far between.

But later, my dad had a sudden cerebral hemorrhage

and passed away. That year, I was in my second year of high school. From then on, my world came crashing down. I lost the only person who truly loved me, and life seemed to have no meaning whatsoever. I was in a coma-like sleep for three or four days and took a leave of absence from school for over two months. Even in my dreams, I was calling out to my dad, begging him to take me with him. It was an incredibly heartbreaking, miserable, and dark period. It wasn't until I went to college that things gradually got better and I started to make my own friends.

Yet, depression has always lingered around me, becoming the dominant hue of my personality: introverted, melancholy, aloof, reclusive, and suppressed... Although I've been working and living diligently and earnestly, sorrow can well up in me at any time and place, and before I know it, I'll sink into disappointment and despair. Even over the tiniest everyday matter, I can spin a whole tragedy in my mind. When in sorrow, all I can think of is: "Die, die. Just go die."

In my memories, I have thought about death more than once, though this is just an estimate. Not far from the entrance of my old home, there was a river. One day, I lingered by its banks for a long time, thinking about jumping in. But it had been raining those days, and the water was murky and gurgling unpleasantly. I thought it over and over again, and in the end, I gave up. Another time, I thought about getting hit by a car. I walked along the road, hoping for the right opportunity, but none came. Later, I considered several ways to end my life, such as jumping off a building, slitting my wrists, or taking sleeping pills. But I never tried any of them. Maybe I was too scared of death, or perhaps it was because none of the methods felt like a perfect or peaceful way to die.

Day can never comprehend the darkness of night. Those around me have no idea how depressed I truly am. There's no point in saying more about it. I just smile and let it pass. I started learning Buddhism more than a decade ago. People around me didn't understand it. They believed that only people who were unhappy with life, or who had seen through the world's vanity, would study Buddhism. Most of the time, I just smiled. But in my heart, I always silently said, "How do you know I'm not unhappy with life? How do you know I haven't seen through the world's vanity?" I watch them eat, drink, play, and have fun. I listen to them chat about all kinds of gossip and news, looking so happy and satisfied. I also want to blend in, but I really find it so boring and meaningless. Happiness, joy, sadness, and pain all seem meaningless, and life itself feels like it has no meaning.

I also tried to embrace life—learning to play ball games, practicing calligraphy, painting, and even studying the tea ceremony. I threw myself into all kinds of activities just to kill time. Yet, at best, such a life could only offer me momentary relaxation. It never really eased the tension in my heart, nor could it truly bring peace to my lonely soul.

I also wanted to try counseling, but I've professionally studied educational psychology, and I understand all those theories. I've also delved deep into Buddhist doctrines. Yet in crucial moments, my sorrow still surges out of control, flooding back like a mighty river bursting its banks.

It wasn't until over two years ago that I met my Master, and encountered his teachings...

I haven't felt this kind of sorrow for a long time. Those gray experiences from the past now feel like memories from a distant age. Even when I listened to Master's latest teaching

Depression for two days and one night straight, my soul wasn't touched at all, and not a single tear dropped. I seem to be on the verge of forgetting those past depressions and sorrows.

Yesterday, while I was transcribing the teachings, suddenly, I heard Master's voice: "Remember, what I say is the Truth. A person who loves others more than he loves himself will never cross paths with depression in this lifetime. Depression will never come knocking on his door, because love is the nemesis of depression—just as light is the nemesis of darkness." —Teaching: "Depression" (July 6, 2023). All at once, the grievances, the sorrows, and the resentments welled up from the bottom of my heart along with the audio teaching. Tears streamed down my face, and sadness swept through my heart, like a lone bird crossing a gloomy sky.

I know, what Master said in the teachings can precisely apply to me. The reason I've been depressed since childhood is that I've always lacked the ability to love. I've been waiting for others to love me. I neither have the ability to love others nor the ability to love myself. Much of my childhood depression stemmed from the feeling that my mother loved my younger brother but not me. In adulthood, my depression has largely come from the feeling that my partner loves his family more than he loves me. The cause of my depression is loss of love, being ignored and overlooked. So, the root cause is that I still love myself.

My Master said, "I have never believed that a person who has genuine love in their heart for others and for society could ever develop depression. That's absolutely not possible, not even 0.001% possibility. It's just impossible. The reason for every single case of depression is that the person has lost the ability to love within their heart." —Teaching: "Depression" (July 6, 2023)

For over two years, I have been immersed in the teachings, bathed in Master's divine love and forgiveness. I understand that life is nothing more than a matter of karmic causes and conditions. I know that all lovers, relatives, and friends are nothing but karmic debts from past lives. I realize that love, hatred, affection, and grudges are nothing more than bubbles in a dream. All of these are just scripts written by my ego, and they have nothing to do with me.

I know that the essence of life is nothing but perfect

love. Self-protection is not true love; instead, it is bondage, confinement, shackles, and a closed loop. For a lonely, fragile, and depressed soul, light alone can shine in, love alone can soothe, forgiveness alone can bring release—and only by letting go and stepping forward can one see the light, feel the love, and become both.

Today, I am a soul deeply loved by Master, a Buddhist disciple deeply cherished by the Tathagata, and a child deeply embraced by the Holy Lord. In such divine love, how could depression possibly exist? When the holy light shines in, the gloom has nowhere to hide and fades away on its own.

So, when they suddenly appeared today, I stopped transcribing the teachings. I looked at them, faced them squarely, and opened my heart to embrace them. I recalled the past with them, watched those sad scenes together, and slowly expressed my heart-ache, understanding, comfort, and embrace to them. When we forgave, pardoned, and blessed each other, we reached a reconciliation, and we pressed our palms together in joy.

Farewell. Goodbye. See them off as you would an old friend.

To all who have suffered from depression, who are currently battling it, or who feel trapped in its darkness, I extend this invitation to you all. Learn to love yourselves, to love others, to cherish every karmic connection, and to embrace every encounter. Bask in the sunlight. Embrace the Truth. Receive Master's blessings. Accept the redemption of the Buddhas and Bodhisattvas. Welcome the grace of the Holy Lord.

This illusory world is not worth your depression. This fleeting life cannot bear the weight of depression. Depression itself is like mist and dew, like a dream or an illusion. Just wave your hand and flick it away—there will be nothing left.

We are the true Spirits, the eternal Love. The radiant Heaven is our true home. There lies the origin of our souls, where we bask in supreme bliss and joy, and are abundantly endowed. Go home, go home, return to the loving home of the soul. It is already filled with divine love. At this very moment, my heart is warm, peaceful, and fulfilled, with no trace of depression.

I forgive you, embrace you, warm you, accept you, and love you.
Merge into my love, and no one can ever harm you.

Cases

HALLUCINATIONS, TREMORS, AND INSOMNIA DISAPPEARED

When I was about eight years old, I suddenly felt as if there were two of me. I stood outside my body, looking at myself and wondering who I was. It felt very strange. At the same time, the people around me also seemed weird and unfamiliar. This feeling came and went intermittently throughout my adolescence. Later, I somehow grew up without really knowing how. Then I felt like I was a plant, having very little connection with the world. I couldn't fit in and felt very lonely. I wanted to keep going, crossing one mountain after another. But when I realized there were still more mountains beyond those ahead, I felt suffocated, as if trapped in an enclosed space. I often imagined flying upward and standing on a high mountain peak, taking in the view. That image brought me relief.

After growing up without really knowing how, starting in 2007, I gradually became more integrated with my surroundings. The childhood dreams and the sense of not recognizing myself gradually faded away.

I got married in 2012. Family life was filled with exhaustion and fear. At work, I was often criticized by my superiors, and I was filled with fear of both going to work and coming back home. In 2016, I got divorced. Every day, I felt like a bird startled by the mere twang of a bowstring. I worried that coming from a single-parent family would negatively affect my child's development. I regretted my past choice. I was afraid of making mistakes at work, getting laid off, and being unable to make a living. I was anxious about not being able to buy a suitable house. I also feared being discriminated against because of my divorce. The work pressure remained intense, and I continued to be met with cold shoulders from my superiors.

In 2017, I constantly felt as if someone were slapping me in the face, and even forcing me to stand at a height and jump off. I was so scared that I dared not go to high places. I suffered from unbearable headaches, experienced memory decline, and felt drowsy every day. I had communication barriers with others, my thinking became muddled, and I was very nervous, always in a flurry. Gradually, I began to feel inferior.

From 2019 to 2021, I faced extremely high work pressure and my mood hit rock bottom. Although the hallucination of being beaten disappeared, I was constantly fatigued and lacked the motivation to do anything. I occasionally experienced hand tremors and suffered from insomnia. Every day felt like the sky was overcast. I had a particular fear of autumn and rainy days, and I always looked forward to spring. I would yell at my child and speak in an extremely irritable manner. This state persisted almost every day. I realized that I was depressed, but I was reluctant to accept it. I didn't go to the hospital for a check-up or take any medication. Instead, I chanted mantras, which had some minor effects. If I chanted continuously, my mood could improve for a few days, but as soon as I stopped, the symptoms would immediately recur.

During that period, my sister introduced Master's Teachings to me, and I studied them off and on. But when I listened to the recordings, I felt completely drained and could barely concentrate. My body felt boneless, and even ordinary sounds felt unbearably loud. Each time my sister patiently guided me, I would grasp a little, but after a few days I would set it aside again.

Now, I have growing confidence in the Truth. I gradually started learning in the second half of 2021, and there was a period this summer when I studied with great dedication. Now, my depression has vanished without a trace. It's as if I had never gone through that period. My heart feels so bright, and my fears have disappeared. Most notably, I'm no longer afraid of going to work. My worries about my child's education and health have also gone away. I've experienced a kind of happiness that I haven't felt for years. I now completely believe in Master. I hope Master will bestow blessings upon me, and I'm determined to study the teachings assiduously!

The soul, emerging from the pitch-black despair, catches sight of light and hope, and experiences a sense of safety and warmth. Once it has these feelings, it finds the way home.

Cases

A 4-Year-Old Boy with Autism: An 18-Month Miracle

In December 2020, a 4-year-old boy with autism was referred here by a pediatrician from * Hospital. At that time, the little boy didn't speak or could only speak incomplete words, and had a blank facial expression, which was typical of autism.

The boy's parents were working in other cities, and the whole family was extremely anxious and worried. I instructed the child's parents to let the little boy listen to *Dream* 24 hours a day.

Today during the follow-up visit, the little boy could communicate normally with others. He recited several ancient poems and actively interacted with the medical staff. According to his parents, he has returned to normal in every aspect. His autism has been completely cured!

To help maintain the progress we've made, the child came

in for a follow-up today. I suggested that the child recite *Dream* regularly over the next three to six months.

A complete recovery from autism in just eighteen months would be seen as a miracle in the medical world. Motivational platitudes alone, or modern medicine by itself, offer limited hope. Only the Truth has the power to reach and heal a child's love-deprived heart.

Cases

A Ray of Hope for Children in Special Schools

(I)

Let me share the reaction of an autistic child after listening to Master's audio recording:

Previously, he would constantly clap his hands, bang on the table, or wave his arms wildly—he simply couldn't stop moving for even two minutes. But when he listened to Master's recitation of *Peace of Mind* for the first time, he actually sat quietly and listened for 2 to 3 minutes! And remarkably, he even shed tears afterward.

I played Master's *To Love* for him. The audio is over seven minutes long. Surprisingly, he lay quietly on my lap, enjoying a massage from me while listening to the audio for nearly ten minutes. After five or six days, he can now listen to it for about fifteen minutes at a time.

This is truly incredible for an autistic child.

We have a device for playing *Dream* at home. I never taught him how to turn it on. One day, he went out to play and came back. The first thing he did was to turn on the player and start listening to *Dream*. After that, he no longer nagged about watching TV. When his mother came back from work that day and saw him not watching TV but quietly listening to the teachings on the trampoline, she thought it was absolutely amazing!

I have him read a short passage from the audio with me every day. Now, he can already read two-thirds of *To Love* with me.

I remember once when he was listening to the *To Love* audio, he suddenly hugged my head with both hands and pressed his head forcefully against mine. Immediately, I noticed a sense of fear welling up inside me, and all the hair on my body stood on end. Wow! I realized I was afraid he would hit me. He sometimes self-harms and sometimes attacks others.

How can we help a child experience love? Acknowledge him more, affirm him more, say "I love you" more often, and hug him more. Try various ways to awaken in his soul the once-familiar experience of warmth and the memory of light.

The moment this thought arose, I immediately brought myself back to a state of mindfulness: I am love and forgiveness. If he really hits me, so be it. I accept everything and embrace everything!

Before I could even react, he pressed his face against mine, first on the right cheek and then on the left. Whoa, I was completely startled. I wrapped my arms around him and patted his back, saying, "Good boy, good boy, good boy!" Then

I softly whispered to him, “You are love. You are not this body, nor the self that identifies with the body, sweetheart. You are love.”

Then a pure, innocent smile spread across his face, and he murmured softly, “You are love. You are love...”

(II)

The child could recognize the Arabic numerals from 1 to 5, but was unable to write them clearly. After class today, I copied down the teacher's homework and asked him to give it a try. To my surprise, when I pointed to the numbers and asked him the questions, he answered every one correctly. Wow, I was totally stunned. It was really amazing!

I quickly took out my phone to record the moment and sent the video to his mother. After watching it, his mother was so excited that she immediately posted the video in her family group chat for her parents and other relatives to see. Everyone praised the little boy and wondered how he had changed so much, as things like this had never happened before.

His mother replied, “Is it because he’s been listening to

the audio recordings from your Master that he's made such progress?" I said, "Yes, I think so. You must have confidence. If you want your child to improve more quickly, you should also listen to and copy the teachings. If parents solve this, the child will improve even faster!"

Since then, his mother has also started to listen to the teachings.

When his father saw the video, he came home that evening and set a few questions for his son to do. The child answered them effortlessly, and his father said happily, "It's as if a switch has been flipped in him."

Such a minor progress means little to a normal child, but it's a cause for great celebration for a family with an child with autism.

(III)

How time flies! More than 100 days have passed in the blink of an eye. This child with autism has changed so much and in so many ways. Let me share a few small examples.

1. Able to Express Hunger and Fullness

In the past, when the little child was hungry, he did not know how to express it and could only cry to show that he needed food. But now, when it's mealtime and he's asked, "Are you hungry?" He can answer, "I'm hungry. I want to eat!" If he's not hungry, he'll say, "No, I don't want to."

In the past, he could neither express when he was hungry nor feel when he was full, so he would keep eating until he vomited, yet still want more. Now, he sometimes touches his tummy and tells me, "I'm full, I'm full."

2. Learning to Go Supermarket Shopping

The other day, I took him to a big supermarket for the first time. His mum told me he used to grab snacks off the shelves in small shops, so the family began avoiding those places and barely even took him to a supermarket.

When we entered the supermarket that day, the staff reminded us that masks were mandatory, and he cooperatively put his mask on right away. I let him push a little shopping cart, and he walked curiously beside me as he pushed it. When we got to the drinks aisle, he suddenly dashed over, pulled out a bottle of beverage, and tried to open it and drink right there. I quickly stopped him and said, "You can put the drink in the shopping cart. We have to wait until the cashier finishes scanning and paying before you can drink it, okay?" He looked at me, replied "Okay," placed the drink back in the cart, and we continued shopping.

We also took him to the playground, and he had a wonderful time that day. His parents were thrilled to see he could go to the supermarket without any problems.

3. No More Spitting

Back in April, he had a really bad habit of spitting everywhere, and sometimes it would land on his classmates or even their parents. Since most of the children in his class also have special needs, the other parents were understanding and never complained.

When I picked him up from school and we waited at traffic lights, I didn't dare stop the car in the middle of the road. I'd always pull over to the side of the street, worried his spit might fly and land on passersby.

I placed a trash basket right next to him on purpose. After a few days, whenever he felt the urge to spit randomly, he'd glance at me. If I stared back at him, he'd turn to the trash can and spit inside. Gradually, it became a habit, and now he instinctively spits into the trash can whenever he has saliva, and there hasn't been a single instance of random spitting ever since!

4. Learning to Enjoy a Variety of Cartoons

When I first met him, he would only watch the *Fruit Hero* cartoon, and he'd keep watching the same episode over and over again. He refused to watch any other cartoons.

Now, after listening to the teachings daily, he's learned to watch cartoons like *Journey to the West*, *Hu TuTu*, and *Big Head Son and Little Head Dad*. When we watch TV together, I explain the stories to him. Whenever he sees Zhu Bajie's silly face after he falls down, he bursts into laughter!

Now, I guide him to say the names of the shows he wants to watch. Before, he could only point with his finger, but now he can name many programs on his own!

5. Can Follow and Read Through *Forgiveness* and *To Love*

Now he can fluently read these two passages with me word by word. Moreover, when I read the first half of a sentence, he can continue with the second half. Initially, he could only focus on audio recordings for a few minutes, but now, if I give him one or two books along with the audio, he'll happily flip through the pages while listening, fully engrossed for an hour or two. His parents have noticed he's become much calmer; he no longer jumps around restlessly like he used to.

6. Able to Read and Write Arabic Numerals

You might think understanding numbers is incredibly simple, but for these children, it's incredibly hard. The other day, I taught him to write the number "1", and it took ages before he managed to write a few squiggly "1"s that looked like worms. When I asked him to write "2", he stubbornly drew a "3" instead.

"Wow, my goodness!" My blood pressure shot up from the stress. "How can he be so dull? He can't even write such a simple '2', something so easy that he still can't manage it?" These thoughts would instantly flood my mind. No, that's not right and I can't let these thoughts take over! At that moment, I silently repeated forgiveness to myself over and over. "Forgiveness doesn't reason with the mind. Forgiveness doesn't reason with emotions!" Just like that, I kept shouting these phrases inwardly.

I took his hand again to guide him in writing "2". Perhaps he was affected by my earlier frustration, because he suddenly became reluctant to write, chirping nonstop in protest. I tried teaching him a few more times, then asked him to write on his own, but the result was the same. Stubbornly, he turned every attempt into a "3", or even a "5". Watching this, my heart churned violently.

I simply took his hand again and shouted aloud: "Forgiveness doesn't reason with the mind. Forgiveness doesn't reason with emotions. When the heart embodies forgiveness, it transcends life and death." I repeated these lines several times, and then tears welled up in my eyes, my heart softened, and I let go of his hand. I told him, "Let's try a different approach."

I guided his hand to trace the number "2" on the wall and he followed beautifully, even managing to draw its shape. Then I asked him to hold the pen and write "2" on his own. Yet again, he wrote "3", "4", or even "6". I checked my heart again; it still rippled, though less intensely. So I continued reciting the "Forgiveness" passage with my whole being, engaging body, mind, and spirit.

Next, I had him grip my finger like a pen to draw "2" on the wall. At first, I pressed firmly to lead, but gradually I loosened my grip, letting him guide my hand instead. Slowly, my heart stilled, and he grew calm. When I finally asked him to hold the pen and write "2" himself, he did it!

Master's audio has an incredible healing power. It can pervade his soul and gradually restore his body, mind, and spirit to health.

Recovery from Critical Illness

MIRACLE

A few days passed in this state. Then one day, I was so bored out of my mind that it suddenly hit me: there was still a box of test strips—test strips for COVID-19 in my basement. It had been sitting there unused for ages. If I didn't use them soon, the whole COVID thing would probably be over. You know me; I'm a very frugal person. Just letting them sit there unused would be a waste, or tossing them out afterward would be a pity. So I thought, "Might as well test myself. See if I've actually got COVID."

Then I thought that since I could not read the English instructions, I would just follow the picture guides on the box step by step. I swabbed my nose with the cotton stick, then dipped it into that solution, swirled it around, and poured the liquid onto the test strip. And then... wowza, it actually showed two lines! Right then, I felt like I'd won the lottery, you know? I was so happy—I'd finally tested positive too. What an honor. Hahaha!

Then, it was just a joke to me. I really took it as a joke. But then, something strange happened. That night, my condition suddenly worsened—it worsened in an instant. Normally, during the previous week, even though I had no sense of taste for a whole week, my body still felt very light. It was as if I was walking without touching the ground. When I walked, you could see my feet moving on the floor, but my body seemed to be floating above it, completely weightless. Even when I was sick and had lost both my sense of taste and smell, my body still had no weight to it.

I got the test results back and confirmed that I was indeed "positive" for COVID-19. Then, that evening, my condition took a sharp turn for the worse. The next morning, I could hardly get out of bed. The soreness and heaviness in my body had intensified ten to fifteen times compared to before

I took the test. Just getting up was a huge struggle. Now I'm really puzzled! Why? I had been fine the day before. I'd been perfectly fine all along—during the ten days from the night I shivered with cold until I lost my sense of taste, I was fine, without signs of any problems at all. So why, why did my condition suddenly deteriorate ten to fifteen times overnight? I could barely crawl out of bed.

Later, I carefully went over everything in my mind: Oh! You should know that I can detach from my conscious mind, thought, memory, and perception. I can be free of my subconscious, as well as the soul of the deliberating mind within my personality. I am not a soul; I am Spirit; I am immortal Life. Therefore, I can see a human soul—the elements that constitute it, the habitual tendencies and subtle thoughts of the subconscious, and what they're thinking. Only then did I uncover the true cause of human death. Thus, today's teaching is a blessing for those in the future who suffer from cancer or terminal illnesses.

Listen up. The reason is that I had mentally "defined" my own condition. I labeled my condition "I've got COVID" and "I'm positive." That's what I mean by "defining". Get it? It's like

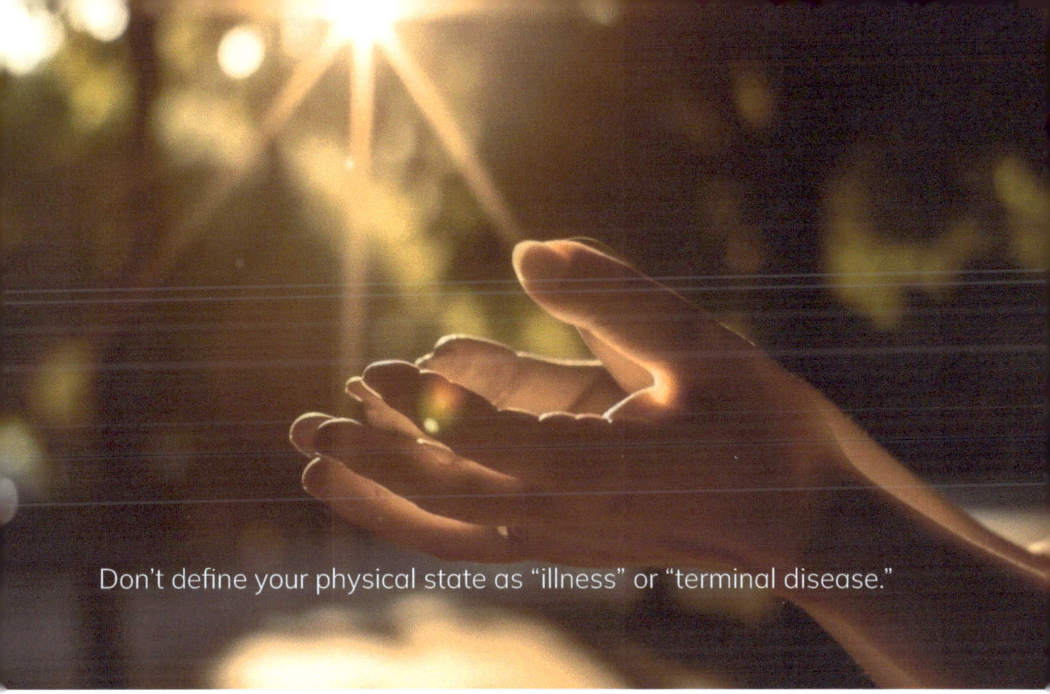

when a hospital labels you: "You're in the late-stage of cancer." Once this is defined, consider: I am already the Divine—a revered, deathless Divine being within the Three Realms. But because my cultivation is not yet complete, those latent habits and subtle thoughts within me are instantly triggered by this "definition". They'll suddenly recall all the memories associated with it. Got it?

"Testing positive" means you're sick, and being sick means your body's functions start failing. It means your karmic obstacles are accumulating. It means your body will manifest the exact state that corresponds to the illness. In an instant, I couldn't even get out of bed. This wasn't something I could control with my conscious will. It was my subconscious at work—those un-purified habits and subtle thoughts within my mind. They're alive. They have memories—memories of life, memories of sickness, memories of death.

So, after more than a day, I listened to the Dharma again, focusing my mind on it. You might think I'm idle and have nothing to do all day, but actually, I'm always listening to the Dharma. You see me watching movies and TV shows every day, but let me tell you, I never turn on the sound when I watch movies or TV series. I only watch those with subtitles. Why? Because I want to listen to the Dharma.

Why do I watch TV while listening to the Dharma? To be honest, it's actually a bit of a laugh. I've listened to the Dharma so much, you know? If there isn't something else to draw my attention, I just can't focus on listening. So, I watch some TV dramas that are quite entertaining but don't require much brainpower—things like gossip, petty squabbles, romantic dramas with lots of "you love me, I love you" stuff. Nothing that needs analysis of the mind.

So I put on my headphones and listened to the Dharma, treating the sound in the headphones as the dialog in the TV dramas. That way, I could actually focus on listening. You know what I mean? I was trying every possible way to force myself to keep my heart, my ears, and my consciousness from drifting away from the Dharma.

I don't aim for achieving a certain state through studying the Dharma. Don't ever think, "I must reach a certain state today." If you think like that, you'll definitely go astray. Just listen. But you must, must make sure to listen for at least six hours. Really, you must. Because it's all about the transition from quantitative change to qualitative change.

In the end, you might not remember a single word, but you're bound to have an experience of peace, clarity, safety, and tranquility. Ultimately, the goal of studying the Dharma is to cultivate this kind of experience. You know? It's about cultivating this sense of peace that objectively exists within your body and mind, independent of your conscious thoughts and the subjective will of your mind.

Then, after listening to the Dharma all day, the experience of peace replaced the discomfort caused by having COVID-19. Instantly, my body returned to normal and felt weightless again. You can see, I still don't have a sense of smell today. You might notice that there's something a bit off with my nose and mouth, as if I have a mild cold or something. I haven't fully recovered yet. I'm still dealing with COVID-19. But right now, my body feels weightless.

Right now, as I'm giving this lecture to you, my body is filled with a sense of radiance. There's no soreness, no stiffness, no chill that usually comes with illness, and certainly no heaviness. It's as if I'm completely free of the disease. Although I outwardly have symptoms like phlegm, a runny nose, and sweating, the internal sense of my body is one of pure, flawless, and weightless radiance.

Well, what I'm going to share with you today is this crucial point: Your illness is "defined" by your subconscious. Seriously, if I hadn't come down with this COVID-19, I wouldn't have known about this. After I tested positive for COVID-19, I endured 24 hours of the suffering typical for patients, lying in bed unable to get up, with my whole body and mind aching and struggling for breath. Then, the moment I forgot about this "definition", my body instantly regained that weightless, radiant feeling, as if my inner self was bathed in light. All I did was replace the heavy feeling brought on by the COVID-related concept in the depths of my heart with the sense of peace I've gained from studying the Dharma. I simply removed this "definition", and all the symptoms disappeared right away.

Then I suddenly remembered something. How old was I back then? There used to be a magazine in China called *Readers' Digest*. You must have read it since you're probably around my age. *Readers' Digest* was one of the major magazines in China back then. As I recall, there were several big-name magazines, like *Good Friends*, *Soulmates*, and *Readers' Digest*. I was around fourteen years old when I read this story in the magazine. It was in the 1980s.

There was an American medical doctor who later went to Africa for exploration. Originally trained as a medical doctor, he changed his career and became a journalist. In the capacity of a journalist, he traveled to the grassland tribes in Africa to explore and learn about the tribe's customs. He lived with the local people in Africa. The whole process took him about three years, during which he accumulated a large amount of notes. After returning to the United States, he published a book, and one of the stories in it was his own personal experience.

When he was traveling across the African savannah with the tribe members, one of the adult males in the tribe fell while chasing prey. He might have tripped over a rock or a wooden stump. His lower-leg bone hit a rock and cracked right open. His leg gave way, and the sharp end of the broken bone pierced through his skin and protruded out. You can imagine, it was a fracture. The bone had gone right through his skin and stuck out from the middle of his lower leg.

Then, a shaman from their tribe accompanied them and attended to the injured man, the one with the broken leg. The shaman treated the wound by mixing herbs they gathered nearby with the menstrual blood of a young woman in the tribe who had just begun menstruating. They then wrapped the leg with a bandage soaked in an ointment, as they called it. After that, the shaman sat beside the patient, gently stroking his head and forehead while chanting incantations and praying for him.

The book records that—the specific time has slipped my mind—after either three days or a week, definitely no more than a week, when the journalist saw the man again—the one with the broken leg, he was already walking and running around nimbly. There was absolutely no sign of the fracture on his leg.

The journalist was absolutely stunned. He said, “This is absolutely impossible.” You know, in Western medicine, this is utterly out of the question. Why? As the saying goes, “It takes a hundred days to heal a bone or tendon injury,” meaning at least three months. We all know that when the body heals a wound with damage and bleeding, it takes about 72 hours, or three days, to recover, and that is not even considering a broken bone.

You’d expect there to be scars after healing, right? He said that when he looked at the man’s leg, he could see on the surface the marks of where it had been broken. But it didn’t look like it had suffered a severe trauma. There were just some healed marks on the surface, nothing more. It was certain that this was the same person, certain that he had been injured, certain that he had suffered a fracture, certain that the bone had pierced through the skin. But now, he was completely recovered. It had taken either three days or a week.

Then he was extremely shocked. He went to ask the shaman

and said, "What's going on?" The shaman smiled and said to him, "This person's bone was fractured because the cells in his muscles and bones were frightened. He forgot his original state of life and showed a look of panic, which manifested as a fracture. What I did was just to make his cells recall their original state of peace. Once he no longer held onto that state of shock, his body recovered."

This incident had a huge impact on me. You know, even to this day, throughout my spiritual practice, I often find myself thinking back to this event. Because what he said was Reality, the absolute Reality. You see, I've lived here for over a decade. Due to my work, about ninety percent of the people I've been in contact with are scientists, professors from various universities. And these aren't just regular teaching professors; they're scientists with their own laboratories, tenured professors.

Many of them, I'd say about seven or eight people I know, work for major pharmaceutical companies. They shared some data with me when I asked how effective the new drugs they develop actually are in curing diseases. Since they're all close friends, they didn't hesitate to tell me the truth.

They told me that drug regulation is extremely strict. From clinical research to administering the drug to patients, each phase requires years of testing. One of the key processes is the double-blind trial. Here's how it works: Let's say we've developed a drug to treat COVID-19. We divide the participants into several groups. In one group of 10 people, 5 take our new drug, and the other 5 take a placebo, which is a pill made of flour with no medicinal ingredients in it. We then tell them it's a wonder drug and ask them to take it. The patients who recover after taking the placebo are basically the same as those who recover after taking our drug.

You wouldn't believe it, would you? A placebo, which is a pill made of nothing but flour with no medicinal effect, can lead to the cure of COVID-19. Let me give you an example. This is called a double-blind trial. In all drug tests, cases where the placebo cures patients account for 20%. Among 10 patients, maybe 5 are cured by the real drug, 2 recover on their own, and 2 are "cured" by the placebo.

How can a placebo, which contains no objective medicinal ingredients whatsoever, cure diseases? It's because the person taking the pill has "defined" it for themselves. I defined it: "This medicine can cure my illness." Do you understand? It's just like how I defined, "I've got COVID-19." Then, in an instant, my subconscious conjured up all the states that should correspond to having COVID-19. If I hadn't made that definition, there would have been no reason for my subconscious to present me with all those symptoms. Do you get it?

My subconscious—those thoughts and habitual tendencies—is not my true self. They form the foundation of my personality and consciousness, but I am not the personality, nor am I the deliberating mind. I have already transcended the deliberating mind; I am the essential Spirit of Life itself. I can observe them, but since I am still... well, I am within them. I can see them clearly, and I am not driven by them. However, I can still be overwhelmed by their collective force. Once they find a reason to coalesce, they form a mental realm that can completely engulf me. Do you understand?

So why can't my mind and consciousness remain continuous in daily life? Most of the time, I'm just eating, playing around, and aimlessly wandering. I continually listen to the Dharma, so that I may abide in a state of conscious Spirit, preventing my habitual tendencies and the perceptions of subtle thoughts from merging with my consciousness. Once they merge, I'll be overshadowed. But when I awaken, they'll be purified by my inner light. It's a process of ebb and flow.

Let me tell you what I mean. If a placebo can cure ordinary patients, then how much more so can those who practice with me. To those in the future, whether you are my students or anyone hearing this today, no matter what diagnosis the hospital gives you, let me tell you that the hospital cannot truly cure you.

Every single scientist around me has a PhD from Harvard, Yale, or similar institutions; every last one of them, without exception. The very least you'd find is someone from Princeton. When it comes to the end of life, every one of them has made it clear: no life-saving measures. They've all signed the paperwork. Absolutely no Western medical interventions, no intubation. Because they come from that world, they are the very ones who developed those tests and treatments. They know exactly what they can and can't do. Don't go for excessive treatment. Please, whatever you do, don't opt for excessive treatment.

Let go of the body. Let go of every label the hospital has used to define your "terminal illness." Place your heart in the Dharma. Place your heart in devotion to the True Divine. The light, the warmth, and the love of the Divine will pierce through the ego and soothe your soul.

The hospital has diagnosed you with a terminal illness, such as advanced lung cancer, advanced stomach cancer, advanced kidney cancer, advanced pancreatic cancer, or advanced melanoma. These are all considered incurable, and that's the label the hospital gives you. But if you choose to learn my teachings, if you are my student, then forget that definition. You can only choose one path.

I encourage you to seek treatment and actively cooperate with it. But deep down in your heart, you should forget that definition. Why? The definition the hospital gives you is not the one given by the Divine. The definition the Divine gives you is that your life is not possible to be ill. It is your body that is ill, and the illness of the body is just a state. And for any state, there is a process of change.

LOVE IS THE MAGIC CURE

The human body arises from the mind; the mind from Spirit; Spirit from Light; Light from Love; Love from Life; Life from Being; Being from Wisdom; Wisdom from Purity; Purity from Peace—and Peace is the heart of Him.

Therefore, when Love awakens in the heart, Spirit awakens. When Spirit awakens within a person, Life awakens. The power of Light within Love would restore body and mind. At the microscopic level of Spirit, the body's cells repair themselves, and human physical diseases, including terminal illnesses like cancer, can be miraculously cured.

Love is the magic cure.
For where there is Love, Spirit abides with the Holy Lord.

Where have all those cancers gone?

Question: Many students who have only been practicing the teaching for a few months, have seen tumors disappear from their bodies. So where have these cancers gone?

Answer: By listening to the audio every day, the cancer cells will be completely eradicated.

Practice and listen to the audio consistently and for long periods.

Within this audio abides the light of the True Divine, the radiance of Spirit, the Compassion of the Buddhas, and the wisdom of the God.

The light carried by the sound can permeate the body, pierce the heart, cleanse the soul, and awaken inner Spirit.

The awakening of Spirit can transcend life and death.

When Spirit is in the awakening process, what happens first

is the revival of Life information within the cells.

As information of Life awakens, that information recalls eternity of Life itself.

Through that information, eternity reveals the warmth of light and love.

Spirit within the cells—in the micro space of Life information—can soothe the cancer cells, melt them, decompose them, and purify them. This is an absolute certainty, and it is something that the Practitioner can be fully assured of and guarantee to achieve.

Cancer cells are the manifestation of the karmic afflictions and evil thoughts accumulated by sentient beings in the lower realms over countless lifetimes. They represent malevolent information.

The audio personally recited by the practitioner arises from the Sages' clear and pure Wisdom, and is suffused with the radiance of Life's primordial Spirit.

Listening to the audio recording is to receive the Divine's purification and deliverance from demonic nature. This is equivalent to the light dispelling darkness within the microcosmos.

It means the soul is redeemed by love in the radiance of the

True Divine.

The power of the Divine can lift the soul beyond the bounds of life and death—how much easier, then, to overcome mere human disease?

Cancer cells are not to be feared; what is truly frightening is a soul that does not recognize the Truth.

When the soul recognizes the Truth, nothing is "impossible" within the Sanctuary.

The Truth itself is a miracle.

Cases

Blindness cured

On the second day after the Qingming Festival in 2018, as I was cooking breakfast, I suddenly noticed that my left eye had gone completely black. Panic surged to the top of my head. I cried out loudly, and my second daughter, son-in-law, and younger sister all rushed out of the bedroom, anxiously asking me what was wrong. I said, "I can't see anything with my left eye. Where are you? I can't see you!"It hit me like a thunderbolt. I felt weak all over, and in my panic, my speech even began to slur. What should I do? What on earth should I do?

I hurried to the hospital. The attending doctor told me I had to be hospitalized. At that moment, I thought to myself: Oh my God, why did you have to make me blind? A perfectly healthy person became a useless person!

In a state of utter panic and not knowing what to do, I asked the doctor how much my eyesight could be restored if I were hospitalized for treatment. The doctor was very straightforward with me and said, “I’ve only encountered this condition once during my previous consultations. You are the second case. You have fundus hemorrhage, which is very serious. I actually didn’t cure the first patient either. For you, being hospitalized is better than staying at home, but I can’t guarantee that I can cure you.” As soon as I heard this, I said, “Doctor, I won’t be hospitalized. If the hospital can’t cure me, what’s the point of staying here?” The doctor replied, “You’re really stubborn!”

The next day, at my family’s insistence, I went to Weifang Eye Hospital, a higher-level medical institution. I registered to see a specialist doctor. The examination results were exactly the same as those from the previous hospital. However, they offered an additional treatment option: there was an injection that could be administered into the eye. Each injection cost 5,000 yuan, and this medication had to be used for two patients simultaneously. If there was no other patient available, I would have to be hospitalized and wait for another patient to show up.

After hearing this, I asked anxiously, “Doctor, if I get this injection that costs 2,500 yuan, can you guarantee it will work?" The doctor replied, "No, I can't guarantee it. We'll have to see how it goes after the injection. If it doesn't work, you may need to continue with more injections." Upon hearing this, my family was stunned. This treatment plan seemed far too risky! At that moment, I was overwhelmed with mixed emotions. There was only one thought in my mind: "It's all over. Both hospitals have given me a death sentence. Not only is my left eye beyond saving, but it might even harm my right eye..."

My family was at a loss, too. Anxiety and eagerness pressed down on us like a dark cloud, almost suffocating us. Meanwhile, the doctor kept asking us whether to go through the hospitalization procedures. At this moment, I felt my Master's voice emerging from the bottom of my heart: "Buddhism is the great King of Medicine. Rely on me, and I'll give you a future!"

These words instantly filled me with strength. Right then and there, I decided not to treat my blindness. I'm going home to heal myself. All the worries, fears, and terrors are useless. Devotion to the Truth is my only choice!

As soon as we stepped out of the hospital gate, we couldn't wait to meet my younger brother and a local senior fellow practitioner. The senior fellow practitioner treated us to a meal. He and my younger brother listed many miraculous cases among our fellow practitioners.For example, one fellow practitioner recovered from a serious illness, and another saw their cancer disappear. The senior fellow practitioner repeatedly said, "The Truth is the great King of Medicine. As long as you believe in our Master, miracles will surely happen!"

After chatting with them for the whole afternoon, my confidence soared. My daughter, still worried, suggested that I go back to the hospital for treatment. I said to my elder daughter, "Mom isn't going anywhere. I still have my right eye in good condition. You all go to work as usual. Don't worry. I'm going to try mind-healing!"

And so, I stopped feeling anxious and instead calmed down to systematically study the Truth. Our Master said, "If our minds are aware and we truly accept the principles that all things arise from conditions and are empty in nature, that the body and mind are like illusions, that there is cause-and-effect and reincarnation, and that karmic retribution is inevitable, then in the midst of suffering, your heart will have no fear and no anger. You'll know in your heart that all sins, sufferings, disasters, and conflicts are the karmic debts from your past life being repaid in this life."

No matter what the situation is, our Master told me, "Accept him, accept him! He is your past self. Even if he wants to kill you, tell him, 'Come and kill me. I'm willing to bear the harm you inflict on me.' Accept him, embrace him, and tell him 'I love you. I understand you.' Open your heart and embrace him with an open heart. Then he will gradually melt away."

Our Master said, "Practicing spiritual cultivation is a process of getting to know your inner self. It means facing your inner troubles and mistakes bravely, truthfully, honestly, and directly. That's what practice is all about. Reveal your troubles and mistakes, repent, expose them, soften them, release them, and let them melt away in the love and forgiveness within your heart. Once those troubles dissolve, the sensations and perceptions tied to recognizing them will dissolve as well."

Through systematic study of the teachings, I've come to realize that all karmic illnesses stem from the boundless

Heaven can restore life to wholeness, for the source of all life flows from the light of the Spirit Heaven.

transgressions committed out of ignorance over countless lifetimes. Therefore, I study the teachings, repent, and practice forgiveness every day. I strive to love all those with whom I have karmic debts from past lives and sincerely ask for their forgiveness. I wish to dedicate the merit and virtue I've gained from my practice to those creditors who have caused my blindness.

Our Master said, "Study the teachings extensively, and miracles will gradually unfold in a heart full of devotion." "Beyond the self in suffering, only the Truth's compassion dwells."

Our Master said, "We must begin by looking directly into our own hearts with courage, and face our true selves. Whenever situations arise, observe what lies beneath the emotions like joy, anger, sorrow, and happiness, and you will find a deep-seated protection of self-interest, such as protecting your image, vanity, desires, feelings, or fear of losing your sense of self. Find this self-protection, then accept it, embrace it, forgive it, and look it straight in the eye. When it gradually fades away, you'll find that the external situations, feelings, the dark fog, the fear, the sadness, and the emotional experiences of joy and pain are like rootless clouds in the sky that simply drift away."

The Master concluded, "In short, it all boils down to one point: all phenomena are created by the mind. Knowing the mind is knowing the one and only Buddha."

Day after day, there were moments when I felt anxious and uneasy, but I never doubted the teachings Master's Teachings.

Whether I was slack or lazy, I always measured my words and deeds against the Truth.

After practicing diligently for over half a year without interruption, one day, I suddenly noticed that my left eye seemed to be able to see things. I immediately covered my right eye, and I could see the table, I could see people! My left eye miraculously regained its sight!

The Truth is truly the great King of Medicine. Miracles have been vividly demonstrated in me. I've benefited from it, and my whole family finds it absolutely unbelievable!

Cases

COMPLETE RECOVERY FROM BREAST CANCER

I'm a 60-year-old breast cancer patient. I underwent surgery in 2018. After chemotherapy, I developed an anxiety disorder. I suffered from memory loss and insomnia, and lost all my hair. The illness ravaged me, leaving me looking like a ghost and turning my life into a living hell. In an attempt to get better, I turned to chanting Buddhist scriptures, but it didn't work. Then I went to see fortune-tellers and had my fortune told, yet the more I tried these things, the more ineffective they proved to be. I've been living like a walking corpse.

It has been a string of bad luck: my daughter got married in her 30s, only to get divorced right soon after giving birth. Her husband, who works out of town, doesn't send any money to support their child. Now she's developed depression. I know she's under immense pressure because she has no job, a baby to care for, and I am also on medication. It is all so agonizing and unbearable!

It never rains but it pours. Around that time, something happened to my husband. Due to a legal dispute involving the protection of personal rights, he was detained for six months and later sentenced to one and a half years in prison, suspended for three years, with the restriction that he could not leave the local area during that period. I won't go into the details, but we felt extremely wronged. What on earth was going on? I really felt like crying , but no tears would come. Why? Why?! I began consulting lawyers and spent over ten thousand yuan on legal fees. The conclusion was that there was no hope for an appeal. As soon as I heard this, I immediately broke down, collapsed to the ground, and my condition worsened. I cried out to heaven and earth, but no one responded. Oh, my God, why was this happening... From then on, I began to feel resentful and angry, full of complaints. How could anyone go on living like this?

One day, I happened to visit a fellow student's home. The fellow student said, "Didn't you read *Dream* I gave you six months ago? If you want to live, you have no choice but to go home and copy and recite *Dream*. If you don't learn our Master's Teachings, you'll definitely end up with dementia.

Who can save you then? Just study it. In less than 10 days, your husband will surely be out."

Finally, hearing these words, I managed to connect with Master. That's when I started copying *Dream*, reading it word by word, writing it down character by character. It was such a painstaking process. After just half an hour of copying, the joints in my fingers hurt so badly I couldn't even straighten them. But then I started listening to Master's audio recordings. After just a few days, my mood suddenly brightened. The heavy, depressed feeling in my heart lifted right away, and my mind gradually became clear. It was truly miraculous. And sure enough, my husband was released in just one week—not even ten days!

Under Master's guidance, my finger healed completely after a month, and my mind grew much calmer, filled with joy and happiness. As I continuously copy the teachings, I don't even remember when my anxiety disappeared, and I'm no longer nervous or fearful. My body has gradually recovered. The hospital had advised me to come in for a check-up every six months, but I haven't gone for a year and a half now. All the symptoms of cancer have vanished. I find it all completely unbelievable and truly miraculous!

My daughter also found a job and is extremely happy every day. My husband is becoming happier and happier too. In the past, the area between his eyebrows looked pitch-black, as dark as soot at the bottom of a pot. He used to curse constantly and was often plagued by violent thoughts. But now, he smiles all the time and seems like a completely different person. He even supports me in copying the teachings. Our whole family has pulled off a "magic transformation"! All of this is thanks to Master's audio recordings played at home. I'm speaking from the bottom of my heart. Without our Master's compassionate blessing, our whole family would have been suffering in hell!

I can never fully repay my Master's boundless compassion. All I can do is immerse myself in the teaching every day, live and die within it, stay true to the Truth, and follow my Master life after life, never leaving or abandoning. Whether in life or in death, I will always be the child of the Holy Father.

Master:

In the future, such miracles will commonly occur. Because

the process of an Eighth-Ground Bodhisattva advancing to a Ninth-Ground is precisely the process by which His holiness begins to descend into the human world, offering compassionate redemption to souls.

Any soul that studies the teachings—so long as it remains devout and chaste—will surely receive His compassionate guardianship. When a mortal soul receives His redemption, it would be truly inconceivable if no miracle appeared in this person.

Miracles are life's natural state.
Death is an unnatural state of life.

Cases

A TUMOR OF OVER TEN YEARS HAS SHRUNK BY HALF

Miracles have finally happened to me. When I received the CT re-examination report from the hospital, I saw that the tumor that had been with me for more than ten years had shrunk by half. I was surprised, but at the same time, I felt it was inevitable, because I truly believe from the bottom of my heart that all the problems are due to not studying the teachings enough. As long as I keep following my kind Master to study the teachings, there is no problem that can't be solved. Sooner or later, this day will surely come. Miracles will surely happen. It's just that I didn't expect them to happen so soon. Maybe it's because our Master has made rapid progress recently, and we have also benefited from it!

Let me tell you about my experience.

In my 36th year, which is considered my benming year (the year of one's birth sign in the Chinese zodiac), I started experiencing discomfort in my body. My entire body became yellowish and swollen, and my skin was extremely itchy. Later, in a full-body check-up, a tumor was found growing in my abdomen. It had blocked the common bile duct, preventing bile from being discharged. As a result, the bile spread to the blood vessels and the surface of my skin. The tumor also began to spread to various organs within the abdominal cavity. I underwent a cholecystectomy (gallbladder removal), a duodenal anastomosis, and a partial gastrectomy (partial stomach removal). However, the doctors didn't dare to remove the tumor because it was located behind the pancreas. They said there were many arterial capillaries in that area, and they were afraid of severe bleeding. Later, when they just removed some of the surrounding tissues, the bleeding couldn't be stopped. I spent 24 hours in the ICU receiving a large amount of blood transfusions. After being out of the ICU, due to a large amount of stagnant blood in my abdomen that couldn't be expelled, I had to apply for another surgery to remove the blood clots. I was back in the ICU, receiving a blood transfusion while having blood drained, with tubes inserted all over my body.

On the third day, I heard the doctor say that if the bleeding couldn't be stopped, there would really be no way out. But by the fourth day, it seemed that the bleeding was finally showing signs of stopping. Eventually, I was able to be transferred out of the ICU. It wasn't until several months later that the last tube was removed.

Later, my husband told me that the night before the bleeding stopped, my life was in mortal danger and he didn't know what to do. That night, he clasped his hands and chanted "Amitabha Buddha" all night. I guess his sincerity moved heaven. In the following months of my recovery, he chanted the Buddha's name every day. Once, he even saw the golden body of Amitabha Buddha, radiating brilliant light and filling him with the joy of Dharma.

Since the previous surgery didn't remove the tumor but only relieved the immediate danger, as long as the tumor continues to grow, my life will be at risk. It's like carrying a time-bomb around with me. The doctor suggested chemotherapy, but I was unwilling to undergo it. I didn't take any medicine either, and I definitely didn't want to have another surgery. So I could only leave it to fate. I went for follow-up examinations from time to time. Fortunately, with the blessings of the Buddhas, there has been little change over the years. In the past year or so, I have listened to Master's Teachings without interruption. Because I have problems with my cervical spine, I rarely copy the teachings by hand, so whenever I can spare time in daily life, I use it to listen to the teachings and read them.

Gradually, I found that I seldom have nightmares. Before I fell ill, I used to have them frequently, and there were times when I was even afraid to sleep. Little by little, I noticed that when I listen to the teachings, read scriptures, or meditate, the whole area of my heart chakra feels warm and hot, and then become cool. When I'm misunderstood, criticized, or insulted by others, I can still manage to be aware of my inner self, and my emotions don't fluctuate much. I can even say I hardly feel anything.

I also have my own spiritual practice method. I often regard my mind as being fully present, observing all feelings, experiences, consciousness, and thoughts at any time and anywhere. It's like watching a movie—where I'm the viewer, immersed in the world on the screen. I am the one watching the movie. I don't belong to this world. I'm here to experience life, but I've just forgotten who I am. Whenever I felt emotionally unsettled, I would quietly observe my inner self and its instinct for self-protection. Through choosing the Truth again and again, I found that my mind gradually became more peaceful.

Below is a comparison of the written reports from my two most recent CT scans:

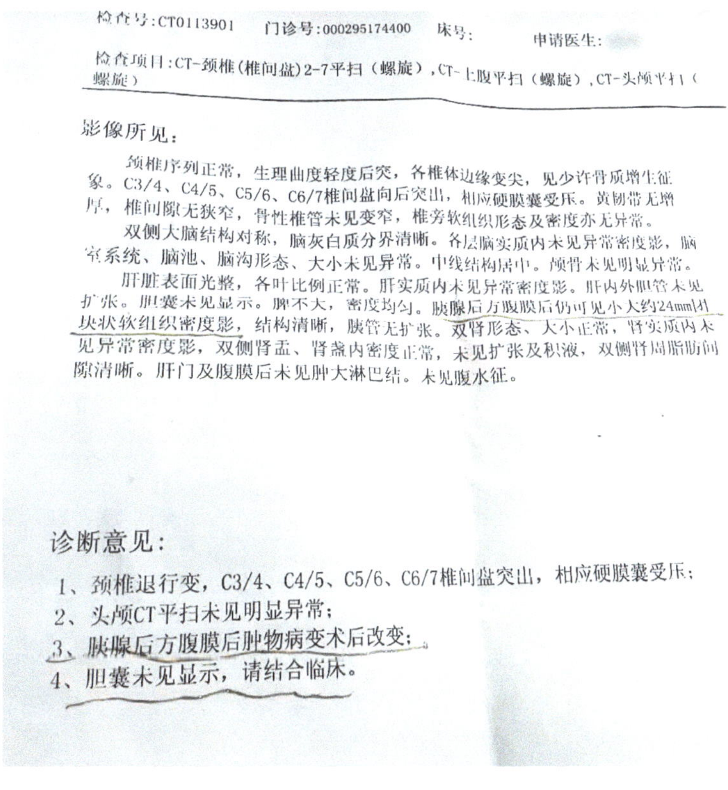

检查号:CT0113901　门诊号:000295174400　床号:　申请医生:

检查项目:CT-颈椎(椎间盘)2-7平扫（螺旋）,CT-上腹平扫（螺旋）,CT-头颅平扫（螺旋）

影像所见:

颈椎序列正常，生理曲度轻度后突，各椎体边缘变尖，见少许骨质增生征象。C3/4、C4/5、C5/6、C6/7椎间盘向后突出，相应硬膜囊受压。黄韧带无增厚，椎间隙无狭窄，骨性椎管未见变窄，椎旁软组织形态及密度亦无异常。

双侧大脑结构对称，脑灰白质分界清晰。各层脑实质内未见异常密度影，脑室系统、脑池、脑沟形态、大小未见异常。中线结构居中。颅骨未见明显异常。

肝脏表面光整，各叶比例正常。肝实质内未见异常密度影。肝内外胆管未见扩张。胆囊未见显示。脾不大，密度均匀。胰腺后方腹膜后仍可见小大约24mm团块状软组织密度影，结构清晰，胰管无扩张。双肾形态、大小正常，肾实质内未见异常密度影，双侧肾盂、肾盏内密度正常，未见扩张及积液，双侧肾周脂肪间隙清晰。肝门及腹膜后未见肿大淋巴结。未见腹水征。

诊断意见:

1、颈椎退行变，C3/4、C4/5、C5/6、C6/7椎间盘突出，相应硬膜囊受压；
2、头颅CT平扫未见明显异常；
3、胰腺后方腹膜后肿物病变术后改变；
4、胆囊未见显示，请结合临床。

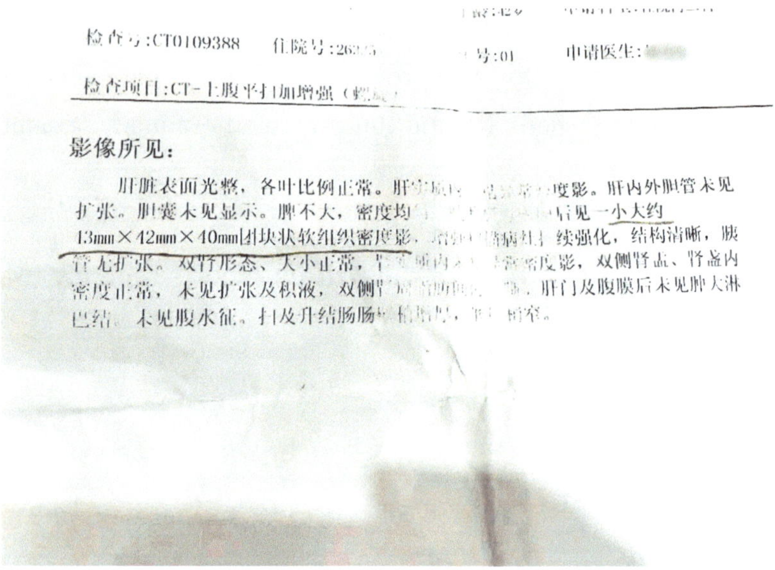

检查号:CT0109388 住院号:26[illegible] [illegible]号:01 申请医生:[illegible]

检查项目:CT-上腹平扫加增强（螺[illegible]）

影像所见:

肝脏表面光整，各叶比例正常。肝[illegible]度影。肝内外胆管未见扩张。胆囊未见显示。脾不大，密度均[illegible]后见一小大约13mm×42mm×40mm团块状软组织密度影，[illegible]续强化，结构清晰，胰管无扩张。双肾形态、大小正常，[illegible]密度影，双侧肾盂、肾盏内密度正常，未见扩张及积液，双侧[illegible]肝门及腹膜后未见肿大淋巴结。未见腹水征。扫及升结肠肠[illegible]

Master: In the eternal light of Heaven, miracles happen all the time, because the Truth is the Divine.

Cases

A PARALYZED ELDERLY PERSON STANDS AGAIN

I am Mr. W, a 71-year-old man living in Yanta District, Xi'an, Shaanxi Province.

Since March 2020, after attempting bigu (a form of fasting) and receiving improper treatment, I've suffered severe damage to my spleen and stomach. They became extremely cold, deficient, and weakened. As a result, my overall vitality declined drastically, leading to poor blood circulation to the heart, frequent high blood pressure, insomnia, heart palpitations, anxiety, excessive sweating, constant fatigue, and an extreme sensitivity to cold. I also developed rheumatoid arthritis in my hands and feet. Eventually, these health issues became so debilitating that I became bedridden and completely dependent on others for daily care. I can no longer eat normal food, so I can only consume porridge that has been blended. I cannot even eat vegetables. I also cannot look at screens, whether a phone or TV, and I find it very difficult to tolerate phone calls or conversations.

In August 2021, fellow practitioner H kindly mailed me books of Master's Teachings, which included *Dream*, *River of Life and Death*, and *Awareness (from 2016 to 2021)*, along with a small audio player, and I felt I had found a precious treasure. Fellow practitioner H also guided me on how to study the Dharma. Following his guidance, I began listening every day to the audio player, which played my Master's own recitations of *The Path* and *Dream*. I started with the very first file and listened all the way through from beginning to end. After that, I repeatedly listened to *Dream*, memorized it, copied it by hand, and practiced repentance. Fellow practitioner H emphasized the importance of repentance, so I followed Master's recorded voice and engaged in repentance every day persistently. I just kept practicing repentance, over and over. Gradually, I increased the amount of time I spent listening to the Dharma and copying the texts. There were even times when I was able to copy the Dharma for about four hours a day.

About six months later, I met a fellow practitioner D, who shared his experience with Buddhist practice. He said that it's best to keep listening to the Dharma even while sleeping at night, with the volume turned very low. After hearing his advice, I began playing my Master's recorded recitation of *Dream* every night while I slept. I'm truly grateful for his guidance.

Strangely enough, in the past, I couldn't stand any kind of noise, whether it was from family, strangers, people talking, the TV being on, or someone calling me on the phone. But when I listen to the audio recordings of my Master's own recitations, such as *Dream*, my heart feels calm. I don't feel irritated or uncomfortable at all. I started with just one hour a day of listening to the Dharma and half an hour of copying it. Gradually, I increased the time to two hours of listening and one hour of copying *Dream*. Now, I'm able to maintain copying the Dharma for about four hours a day.

Since I started following my Master's Teachings, my health has gradually improved and I'm slowly recovering. I can now eat normally again, including vegetables. I can walk downstairs with the help of my wheelchair for exercise, and I'm up to walking over a thousand steps a day.

This summer, I stopped using my wheelchair and began walking with it just as a support. Then, starting last month, I didn't even need the wheelchair at home anymore, and I can now walk around using just a cane. Sometimes, I can even help my spouse do chores like washing dishes, sweeping the floor, and preparing vegetables. The speed of my recovery has been truly unbelievable. If I hadn't practiced my Master's Teachings, I probably wouldn't be alive today; I might have been long dead by now.

I never imagined that a dying patient who was paralyzed and bedridden could ever stand up again, let alone walk and even do a little housework. This is all thanks to the compassionate power and blessings of my Master's Teachings.

May everyone in the world receive the salvation and grace of our revered Master.

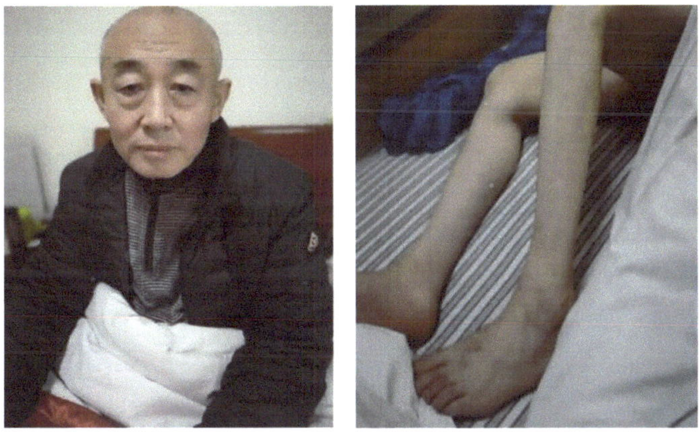

Photos of me during my serious illness, before I began practicing the teachings

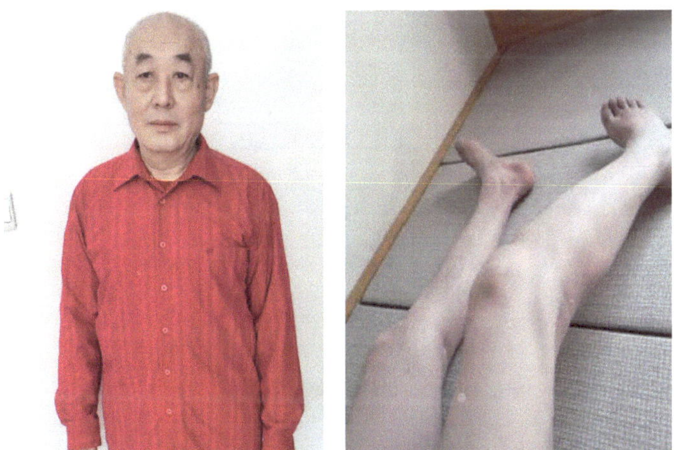

Photos of me in recovery, after one year of practicing the teachings

Cases

A 40-YEAR CHRONIC HEADACHE HAS BEEN CURED

Since the release of my Master's teaching *Spiritual Resonance*, I have been listening to it around the clock. I believe that the Teachings the Master gives now carry even greater blessings and power than those from the past. After listening continuously for ten days, I noticed two clear changes:

1. The stubborn headache that tormented me for nearly forty years is completely gone, so I'm healed at last! I've had it since I was just 12 years old. I tried every treatment imaginable and took handfuls of painkillers every day. My coworkers even said I was addicted. But now, for the past few days, the pain has completely disappeared, and I don't even remember to take the pills anymore. Just three days after I started listening to *Spiritual Resonance*, the pain stopped. At first, I did not quite believe it and wondered if it could really be true. But the sensation in my head has been completely new and refreshing, bringing a cool, calm feeling I have never felt before, and this

When you receive the Divine's blessings and love, and are warmed and purified by the Light, the pain in your body, the conditions you suffer—as you let go of the painful memories—can grow lighter day by day, until they heal completely.

has lasted for six or seven days now. No medicine. No pain. This has never happened before. It's real. It's truly real.

2. The lighter, happier, carefree, and sunny side of me is taking the lead. Although the old personality patterns and habits still pop up from time to time and cause a bit of trouble, they are growing weaker and no longer have the power to take control. It's like there are two people inside me: one is full of positive energy, joy, and light; the other is weighed down by heavy negativity. Every time that negative energy shows up,

before I even have time to fully feel it, it is gradually dissolved and melted away by the brighter, more joyful, and more uplifted side of me.

Incredible! I couldn't hold back my tears—utterly shaken and moved.

Cases

A 10-CENTIMETER OVARIAN CYST HAS DISAPPEARED

During the clinical examination, the ultrasound doctor couldn't believe that I'd had a 10-centimeter ovarian cyst three years earlier, and said, "It would be very difficult for it to disappear without surgery." I replied, "You can check because I had an examination here before. If you don't believe me, you can look it up in my medical records."

She checked the computer and confirmed that a 9.6-centimeter ovarian cyst had been detected in my previous examination. Then she asked, "How did that happen?" I replied, "I've been practicing Buddhist Teachings. My state of mind has improved, and through the purifying power of the Dharma, the ovarian cyst naturally disappeared. Practicing the Dharma has made me truly happy!"

To substantiate the profound changes I experienced from simply practicing my Master's teachings on devotion and forgiveness, and to inspire greater confidence in fellow students who are just beginning their practice, I'm not afraid to share my privacy, so here are copies of my actual ultrasound reports!

My family knows I've been running long distances for 20 years, but even that didn't help with the ovarian cyst. I never underwent surgery to remove it either. The only explanation? It's nothing short of a miracle and is a clear manifestation of the power of my Master's Teachings.

These ultrasound reports are, in fact, powerful evidence for my family members who do not believe in the Buddhist Dharma or in the power of my Master's Teachings.

The attached images are the ultrasound reports from these past years, presented in chronological order:

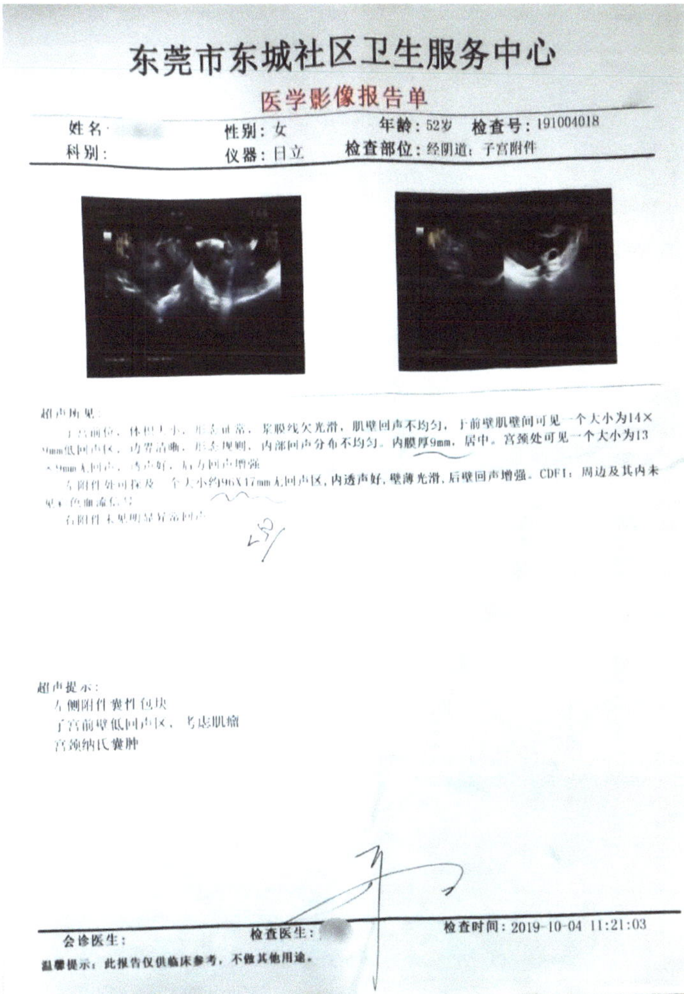

东莞市东城社区卫生服务中心

医学影像报告单

姓名： 性别：女 年龄：52岁 检查号：191004018

科别： 仪器：日立 检查部位：经阴道：子宫附件

超声所见：

子宫前位，体积大小，形态正常，浆膜线欠光滑，肌壁回声不均匀，于前壁肌壁间可见一个大小为14×9mm低回声区，边界清晰，形态规则，内部回声分布不均匀。内膜厚9mm，居中。宫颈处可见一个大小为13×9mm无回声，透声好，后方回声增强

左附件处可探及一个大小约96X47mm无回声区，内透声好，壁薄光滑，后壁回声增强。CDFI：周边及其内未见彩色血流信号

右附件未见明显异常回声

超声提示：

左侧附件囊性包块

子宫前壁低回声区，考虑肌瘤

宫颈纳氏囊肿

会诊医生： 检查医生： 检查时间：2019-10-04 11:21:03

温馨提示：此报告仅供临床参考，不做其他用途。

2019: Left ovarian cyst measuring 96 × 47 mm, and a uterine fibroid measuring 14 × 9 mm

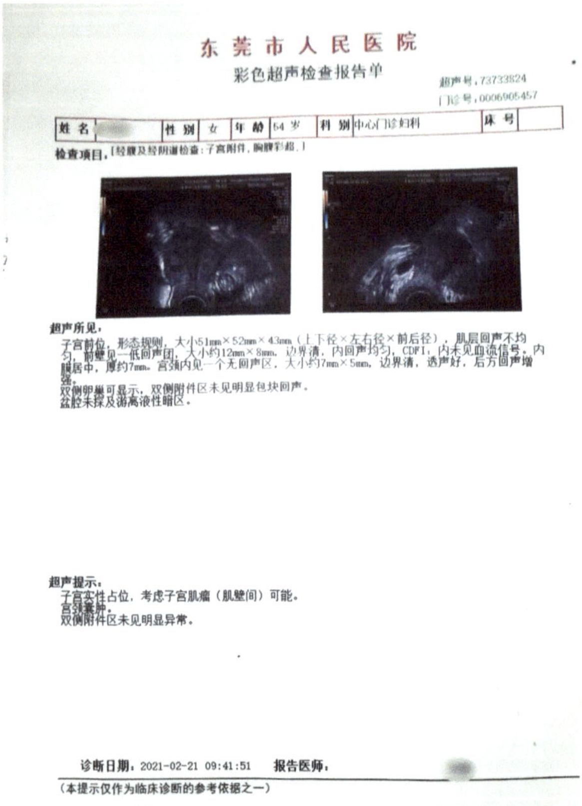

东莞市人民医院

彩色超声检查报告单

超声号，73733824

门诊号，0006905457

姓名		性别	女	年龄	54 岁	科别	中心门诊妇科	床号	

检查项目，[经腹及经阴道检查：子宫附件，胸腹彩超，]

超声所见，

子宫前位，形态规则，大小51mm×52mm×43mm（上下径×左右径×前后径），肌层回声不均匀，前壁见一低回声团，大小约12mm×8mm，边界清，内回声均匀，CDFI，内未见血流信号。内膜居中，厚约7mm。宫颈内见一个无回声区，大小约7mm×5mm，边界清，透声好，后方回声增强。

双侧卵巢可显示，双侧附件区未见明显包块回声。

盆腔未探及游离液性暗区。

超声提示，

子宫实性占位，考虑子宫肌瘤（肌壁间）可能。

宫颈囊肿。

双侧附件区未见明显异常。

诊断日期，2021-02-21 09:41:51 报告医师，

（本提示仅作为临床诊断的参考依据之一）

2021: The ovarian cyst had disappeared. The uterine fibroid measured 12 × 8 mm.

(I had shared this before on social media, and some people questioned the reliability of the smaller hospital's test results. So I specifically went to the most authoritative hospital in the city to have the examination repeated.)

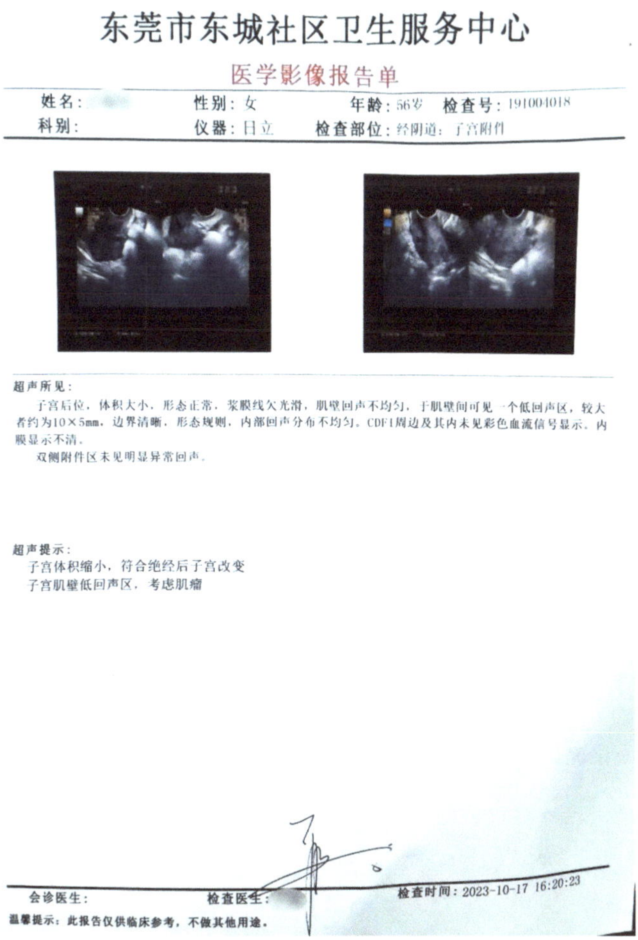

东莞市东城社区卫生服务中心

医学影像报告单

姓名：　　　性别：女　　　年龄：56岁　检查号：191004018

科别：　　　仪器：日立　　检查部位：经阴道：子宫附件

超声所见：

子宫后位，体积大小，形态正常，浆膜线欠光滑，肌壁回声不均匀，于肌壁间可见一个低回声区，较大者约为10×5mm，边界清晰，形态规则，内部回声分布不均匀。CDFI周边及其内未见彩色血流信号显示。内膜显示不清。

双侧附件区未见明显异常回声。

超声提示：

子宫体积缩小，符合绝经后子宫改变

子宫肌壁低回声区，考虑肌瘤

会诊医生：　　检查医生：　　检查时间：2023-10-17 16:20:23

温馨提示：此报告仅供临床参考，不做其他用途。

2023: The ovarian cyst was no longer present. The uterine fibroid measured 10 × 5 mm. (The uterus had also become slightly smaller, making the fibroid negligible.)

Rebirth in Love

Begin by Forgiving Yourself Who Was Hurt

Let's say you run into your enemy right now, for instance. What we call an "enemy" must be someone you know well. Someone you barely know, or a stranger who offends you wouldn't typically be called an enemy—that would just be a minor issue, and you can easily forgive and let go. A real enemy must be someone you know, someone familiar to you, someone you've had interactions with.

Whenever you think of him, even if he is not around, you feel a surge of resentment in your heart. This kind of rising anger—the clenched-teeth, seething feeling—lingers in your mind, leaving you brooding and indignant. At this moment, you must find the motive behind the indignation you feel toward him: Why? Why do you feel such hatred toward this person? Then, you'll probably come up with a long list of reasons: He was unreasonable, arrogant, selfish, even vicious.

Remember this: now is the moment for your to practice my path of forgiveness. The person outside doesn't really exist—he is not in front of you right now. What exists now is only your memory of him within your mind. Behind that memory, there must be cognition. Behind that cognition, there must be an intention. Without intention, cognition would not take shape. So what is that intention behind the cognition? That intention behind—it is, it is, it certainly is—a defense of your self-perception.

Because he was unreasonable, he hurt my self-esteem; because he was greedy, he harmed my interests; because he was malicious, he violated my moral values; and because of his shamelessness and cruelty, he undermined the value of life that my personality holds dear. Therefore in my mind, he takes on the image of a vicious, selfish, shameless, and cruel person. But this image, in truth, is a projection of compared memories by my personality.

If there were no memory of moral values within my personality, I wouldn't know whether he was shameless. If there were no fear of self-preservation within my personality, I wouldn't recognize that his words and actions were meant to harm me. Because when I don't have a sense of the self, I don't perceive anyone's behavior as being directed at me. Do you see what I mean?

Only because I am holding an ice cream and about to eat it do I notice and start to wonder if the person coming toward me might try to grab it. But if my hands are empty and I am not holding anything, then I have no idea what that person intends to do.

Do you see what I mean? That is to say, the enemy in my mind is merely a realm projected by the sense of self-preservation within my mind-consciousness. If there were no defense of my own interests, values, and feelings within me, there would be no one outside who could harm me, nor any deeply ingrained memory of someone who had harmed me.

Therefore, what I truly need to forgive is my own

perception of the person who hurt me. In other words, you need to forgive yourself—forgive the part of you that felt frightened, hurt, and pained by this person, and entrust that pain in your heart to Heaven. He belongs to Heaven. He is safe. No one can ever take away your true Life. What people take away is merely an illusory realm within this space and lifetime, unfolding from past causes and subsequent conditions.

Everything you see is a realm; everything you feel, everything you experience—all are merely realms formed by your deliberating mind and habitual tendencies. Where there are realms, a self arises within them, clinging to those realms. And because there is a self, an enemy arises, who seems to be trying to harm you.

So when this realm arises, you must turn inward and observe the sense of fear that defends your ego—and embrace it in your arms. "The Lord loves you. You are loved by the Lord. You are safe. The Lord loves you." Tell yourself again and again. Then, speak to that wounded part within you—the part that has tried to hurt you and has already suffered deeply: "I forgive you. I forgive you. I forgive you."

At this moment, if you truly don't have the strength to forgive the enemy within your heart, begin by forgiving the part of you that was hurt by him. Embrace that self, cherish him, understand him, warm him with kindness, and love him. Hold that wounded, fearful self of yours in the embrace of your faith. Within your faith abides the Divine, the Lord of Heaven, who is infinite Light, boundless love, eternal warmth, and the immortal, unchanging Life. He loves you freely and unconditionally; He loved you in the past, He loves you now, and He will love you forever. In His love, you are safe. His love for you is unconditional, embracing you without distinction or difference.

You are one with Love. Begin by loving yourself. Let your love, the Life-Love of Heaven, the infinite, radiant warmth nurture the part of your heart that has been hurt by others. Place that fearful, wounded heart within you, the one that has been hurt, scarred, contracted, and in pain, into the infinite, pure, radiant Love.

That Love is your true home; that Love is the essence of your life; that Love is the Lord's unconditional acceptance of you, His endless care and embrace. Let your heart rest in the warm and radiant love of the Lord. When your heart, held in the warmth of love, absolute safety, and tenderness, awakens a healthy, pure smile within you, you will find the strength to forgive the memory of the enemy within. And then, you say to him, "I forgive you. I pardon you." Say it ten thousand times.

TRUE LOVE ARISES FROM THE SOUL'S SELFLESSNESS

Love is not an expression; love is a state of being. Now, let me share a feeling with you. Each of you has experiences in life, in yourself, in the life you've lived. You all carry memories of those experiences. Have you ever felt it—when you love someone, from deep within your heart arises a feeling of happiness and sweetness, a feeling that is light, pure.

This kind of feeling emerges when you love your child. When you hold your newborn daughter or son in your arms, there arises within your heart a wish to give unconditionally, to take on everything for them. That wish holds no emotional waves of romantic love, yet it is deeper and more profound—a kind of acceptance that comes from the very essence of your soul and life.

And then, there's the love you feel when you love your parents, or when you wish to repay the kindness of someone

With the purest love in life, bless others;
With the purest selflessness from the depths of the soul, forgive others;
With the warmest understanding of the heart, accept others.

who has been your benefactor. With a heart filled with gratitude, you hold the wish to give to him unconditionally—to brave boiling water and fire for him, to spare no effort, to risk life and limb, to give yourself utterly without hesitation or complaint. That wish, too, is love.

Then, there is another kind of love—a love that each of you in your life has experienced to some degree, consciously or not: It is helping others without expecting anything in return.

You see a person fall to the ground—this is someone you don't even know—and all the vegetables he was carrying scatter across the road. The traffic around is busy and chaotic, looking dangerous. Yet, without caring for your own safety, you run over to help him up, pick up the things that fell on the ground, brush the dirt off his clothes, and gently guide him to sit down by the side of the road.

At that moment, you didn't think about being falsely accused, getting hit by a car yourself, or whether your own life might be in danger. You simply wanted—with all your heart, purely and sincerely—to help that person out of danger, to rescue them from harm, without expecting anything in return, or any thought of protecting yourself. This instinctive, almost unconscious act of kindness, too, is love.

This love doesn't bring to you emotional turbulence. This love brings to you...Recall carefully for yourselves—when you help others unconditionally and selflessly, without asking for anything in return and without putting up any self-protection, there arises within you a deep sense of joy and comfort, a feeling of peace and gladness. Remember, this sense of peace and joy—that is the love of your soul.

The love of the soul is a giving without asking for anything, without any self-protection. This kind of love is akin to heavenly love. The essence and core of love must be selflessness. Anything with selfishness cannot be called love.

Today, I saw a woman who was incredibly beautiful, with a curvy figure, standing over six feet tall, her skin so fair and smooth it was like egg white. She was absolutely stunning, the kind of beauty that could make the flowers blush and the moon hide in shame. The moment you saw her, you felt this overwhelming urge and are not even ashamed to say it bordered on something reckless. You thought you were in love with her, head over heels, so crazy that you couldn't sleep at night. You took handfuls of sleeping pills, but nothing could ease the longing you felt for her. That wasn't love. That was desire.

The day you see that woman with another man, you feel

jealousy and hatred rising up inside you—anger born from what you thought was love—to the point where you wish you could disfigure her, or even harm the man she's with. That is not love. That is ego-driven desire.

True love does not dwell on names and forms; true love is detached from all names and forms; true love arises from the selflessness of the soul, from that purity of selflessness. Only this purity of selflessness can awaken the soul's memory of Heaven—and the memory of Heaven is none other than selfless love, pure love, eternal love, unconditional love. Love—that is Heaven.

ONLY WHEN YOU LOVE YOURSELF CAN YOU LOVE OTHERS

Student: I feel burdened by heavy karma, and my heart feels empty of love and warmth.

How can I allow my inner self to be filled with love and warmth?

Master: Love yourself. Forgive yourself. Let your heart awaken to warmth and peace within love itself. Learn to cherish and care for yourself—for only then can you truly love others. Love is a practice. It is found through empathy and understanding, through embrace and warmth, and through forgiveness and giving, through acceptance and gentleness.

You are loved by the Lord

Student: I'm truly grateful to you, Master. I struggle with a strong sense of anger and hatred, a strong urge to defend myself, and a lot of fear. Please, Master, could you offer some guidance.

Master: All that you go through in this life is the fruition of causes and conditions from your past lives. Because in your past life you were a steward, and you treated your former subordinates—those servants, maids, and hired workers—very harshly.

Therefore the karma will come to fruition in this life.

I don't have any special advice for your spiritual practice. You just need to learn to love yourself. Your heart is suffering so much. What I see in you is that you are soaked in a pool of bitterness. There has never been a moment when you've felt happiness. You've always been subjected to grievance, blame, injustice, insults, and unwarranted scolding and denial—

and you have grown used to it. Thus your heart is filled with grievance and darkness, with an unwillingness to accept and a sense of helplessness—a blend of resentment and powerlessness.

You must believe: "The Divine loves you. The Lord loves you." So you must also love yourself the way He loves you. This is the spiritual lesson of your life. All right. Go and love yourself. The Divine loves you. Just remember this: "The Lord loves you. He always loves you. No matter what you've done wrong, His love is always with you."

You must find His love deep within your heart and body. That is your spiritual practice. Okay, it won't mean much if I say too much to you. "The Lord loves you!" Well then, just remember this word.

The Lord is love. The Lord loves you.

Unfailing Love, Everlasting Acceptance

Every time you feel the urge to rebel or rise up in defiance, behind that impulse is a soul that has lost love and is trying, through that conflict, to find the safety it is missing.

You mistakenly believe that intensity, rage, and anger, represent power. In truth, what you long for most deeply in your subconscious is warmth and peace that never change and never leave you.

What you truly long for is simply "unfailing love, and everlasting acceptance."

If your soul genuinely feels deep, rich love that never changes, you would never need for vivid release of temperament.

Because when the soul is no longer lonely, no longer afraid, no longer secretly sorrowful—when it is embraced in warmth

The nature of love is trust, safety, selflessness, giving, and sharing of joy and peace. It is taking responsibility without selfish motives. It is an unconditional embrace. It is warm, pure acceptance that comes from deep within the heart.

and peace, when it is joyful and radiant—you are unable to feel the ugliness or harm of the outside world. Even if you witness injustice or see the filth of reality, your response will still be calm and gentle. Because true warmth and love can never be altered by external conditions.

Cases

THE ABANDONED ME, WALKING FROM SHADOW INTO LIGHT

When I was four, my parents divorced. Right in front of me, they said they didn't want me. I cried endlessly every day. My grandfather, out of kindness, raised me for years, but he passed away when I was in fifth grade. After that, I went to live with my grandmother, who was very harsh and critical toward me. My aunts were also sharp-tongued and judgmental, constantly blaming me.

After my mother remarried, I only got to see her briefly on weekends. She was hot-tempered, easily angered, and struggling with mental health issues. She would often suddenly lash out at me over the smallest things, and she wouldn't let me cry.

She would show care for me for only a few days, and then become extremely critical, full of disdain and blame. Her moods were unpredictable, and she treated me like an emotional punching bag.

I've been living under the shadow of abandonment, always feeling like the whole world had given up on me. I was consumed by guilt, shame, and fragility, unable to face reality. The constant accumulation of blame, cruelty, and fear eventually took its toll. Three years ago, after experiencing a series of devastating blows, I completely lost my ability to function at work. My heart closed off completely. I could only lie in bed all day, unable to do anything. Most of the time, I was mentally foggy, unable to speak, and suffered from loss of appetite. My mind was filled with images of the people around me wanting to hurt me. I was in extreme panic, terrified of being harmed.

After encountering the Truth, I came to understand that it wasn't me who was lacking love, feeling wronged, or in pain. No one in the outside world ever truly harmed me, and nothing that happened was ever real. It was all because I had forgotten love, forgotten my true self, and fallen into fear rooted in self-preservation.

When fear, hatred, despair, or panic arises within me, I recognize it and say to it: "You are not me. I forgive you. I

With the warmth deep in your heart,
extend empathy and forgiveness to your personality self.

no longer defend you. I trust only the Divine—not you. The heart of the Divine is my true heart. I surrender myself to the Divine's protection, and I no longer try to protect myself. I love you. I forgive you. I release you. I bless you."

Gradually, my heart began to calm down. With a heart full of empathy and understanding, I communicated with the dark memories within me—the bitterness, coldness, hatred, selfishness, and more. I used the teachings I've learned to cleanse their mistaken beliefs, and listened to the teachings to soothe their fear and tension.

After practicing forgiveness consistently for over a year, I am now able to work from home. Through studying the Truth, I have re-established right values, regained a sense of safety, and achieved emotional stability. I've learned to accept reality as it is, no longer avoiding it, and I now have the inner strength to handle life's challenges.

Now, I often feel a powerful force of light penetrating my body from the back of my head. My heart is no longer weak or powerless—it is filled with strength and positive energy. Every day, I feel the presence of the Divine with me. My heart grows more and more peaceful and serene, often accompanied by warmth and a deep sense of safety. Sometimes, I experience immense happiness and endless fulfillment.

The external world is like a thin sheet of paper. The human world is dry, empty, devoid of true meaning, and unreal. Yet that immense happiness feels profoundly real.

Cases

THE GRIEF AND PAIN OF WIDOWHOOD, REPLACED BY LOVE AND FORGIVENESS

Looking back on most of my life, I realize its backdrop has been hardship and weariness.

The greatest pain of my life was the passing of my husband. He was 33, and I was 30. In April 1995, he was diagnosed with lung cancer, and that was when suffering began. He was my everything. I loved him more than anything in the world. When he fell, my whole world collapsed. I watched helplessly as the illness consumed him, until he was gone. I was powerless and torn by helplessness, despair and grief. My heart ached as if bitten by a cat, and my blood seemed to drip away drop by drop until I felt I was dying inside.

I often found myself alone, staring blankly at the sky, muttering to myself: “Why is this happening? He was fine, so how could he just be gone like that?” It felt like a bad dream

I couldn't wake up from. It was too hard to accept. If we are all going to die anyway, then what is the point of living now? "Forever" turns out to be so short. Money really doesn't matter at all in the face of death. Nobody can give me an answer.

After my husband passed away, I became like a walking corpse—I lost all passion for life, buried all pain deep inside, pretended to be strong, and got through more than twenty years with my son. The experience of hardship and weariness has stayed with me all along.

After experiencing the pain of separation and death, I developed a deep fear of "illness" and "death". I feared getting sick, suffering through a painful death, and even more, the torment of anguish. I wanted to escape to a place where there was no suffering.

That's when I encountered the cult known as Falun Gong. Its promises of "never suffering" and "forever remaining human" seemed to fit my desperate needs at the time. I clung to it tightly, afraid to let go, convinced I had found the Truth. Little did I know, that's when these twisted views took root in my mind. I slandered the Buddha, slandered the Dharma, distorted the teachings of Buddhism, clung to illusions as if they were real, and kept striving for something I could never attain. The more I pursued it, the more elusive it became. I lived each day trapped in fantasy and fear, suspended in a state of neither peace nor liberation, and I was utterly exhausted in body and mind, a pitiful sight to behold.

It wasn't until 2015, when I met my Master and encountered the Truth, that I finally realized I had found the true Dharma. I knew that only my Master could bring me salvation. I stopped searching everywhere and committed myself wholeheartedly to following him. I have never turned away. With an insatiable thirst, I study the Dharma and put it into practice. I dare not slacken in my efforts and cherish every moment with deep gratitude.

"Pain is our inner resistance."—*Acceptance (Part I)* (April 18, 2016)

"Practice, ah, your whole life is but a lifetime of your mind conversing with the self. There is no one else out there. The world is but an illusion. Spiritual practice is a lifelong dialogue deep within the mind—between the discriminating consciousness and the illusions it perceives."—*First Light*

(August 25, 2015)

"With love, dissolve the self; with love, forgive all wrongs; with love, embrace karma; with love, dispel fear. For when the self is dissolved in love, that is liberation.

With love, encompass the world; with love, hold suffering in your arms—that is liberation. When love in the heart melts away the self, there is no division between others and me. All beings and I are one in light."

"Do not turn away from the real world. The world you see is nothing but a projection of the habits and memories deep within your mind. When we embrace our inner world, we treat the outer world with kindness. When we accept and embrace the outer world, we are embracing the lonely soul deep within our heart."—*The Creator—The Great Love* (October 30, 2014)

It was those sacred words from Master's Teachings that dissolved my doubts.

Gradually, I came to accept my resistance, my fate, and my pain... The pain I had carried in my heart for so many years was released and let go of little by little.

And then, one day, I finally understood: everything I had

gone through was the love of my Master. As long as I walk the path to liberation, everything is the blessing of the Buddhas and Bodhisattvas. Only the Truth can truly set all this free. Only the Divine has such power!

In September 2022, I happened to retire, and suddenly had plenty of time to immerse myself in the Dharma, but I forgot that I was once a member of a cult.

"For souls who have cursed the Divine and the Buddhas, studying vast quantities of the Dharma is nothing more than scratching an itch through one's boots. It has no effect whatsoever in purifying their body and mind or awakening their spirituality. The karmic sins of these souls are far too deep, far too heavy."

"Even with the same amount of practice time, the same intensity of studying the Dharma, and the same opportunity for divine salvation, former cult members have an inner state that's worlds apart from that of ordinary people.

No matter how arduously a cult follower studies the Dharma, no matter how hard they try, how devout they appear, how actively they spread the teachings, or how much they confess and practice repentance, their soul still struggles to resonate with the Truth, and finds it almost impossible to awaken genuine joy, gratitude, or heartfelt excitement.

Cult followers may interpret the True Divine's teachings through the distorted lens of their cult beliefs, examining them only to see what personal benefits they can gain."—*Post This as a Testimony* (September 18, 2022)

Yes, I was like this without realizing it, so caught up in names and forms. I thought I was practicing love and forgiveness, but it was all happening in the mind—trying to rationalize my afflictions and desires. "He's had a hard time too, so I should forgive him." That was bottling it up, swallowing your pride, the self forgiving the self. How could that ever lead to true forgiveness? That's why I've felt so exhausted. These old experiences, they never truly melt away. They keep resurfacing, triggered by the slightest thing, pulling me back in. And so I've remained stuck in this cycle, unable to break free.

"Within the body and mind of a cult follower, there is not

the slightest trace of light.

Their inner experience is hard, cold, fearful, anxious, cruel, vicious, selfish, evil, hateful, and dark.

Because they believe and accept the lies of the cult organization, the inner experience of the self is driven by desire. Cult followers crave for themselves to become Buddhas. Their thoughts and intentions are governed by self-centered desires, looking to maximize their own personal ego and interests. Under the influence of greed and craving, their souls are shaped into feelings of arrogance, cruelty, evil, and utter contempt for others."—*Post This As a Testimony* (September 18, 2022)

Master's words are a true reflection of my state.

Once I truly realized it in my heart, I began to take action by making a great vow, praying for my Master's blessings, and committing to breaking free from cultic views in this lifetime and establishing right view. When I compared our Master's Teachings with Falun Gong cult's doctrine, it became clear: all those frozen, distorted inner experiences caused by cultic views were illuminated by the light of the Truth, and I received redemption from the True Divine.

“Only the penetrating light of the True Divine, along with His wisdom and mighty power, can destroy the sins that enshroud the soul, which are as vast and dark as clouds blotting out the sky. It can break through the immeasurably thick karmic obstacles that envelop the soul, thick as the fog of the void itself. And in doing so, it allows the soul to catch a glimpse of the light of Heaven.”—*Post This As a Testimony* (September 18, 2022)

Master's words are truly real and unerring!

On January 1st, 2024, through a conversation, I finally discovered that “seeking mind” within me: it suffers when it cannot obtain what it wants, fears losing what it has, and becomes exhausted and filled with complaints after years of effort without the expected rewards.

Studying the Dharma with wrong views is all futile because the direction is wrong, and my heart just collapsed. I was so afraid of losing Master's protection that I became paralyzed with fear, and my whole body went weak. And in my desperate pursuit of the Truth, I burned the candle at both ends, never daring to relax, until I was driven half-mad with exhaustion.

These experiences came one after another, and I chose to face them truthfully. As I did, the Dharma revealed itself to me, and following that thread, I traced the root of these experiences to the desire to gain and the fear of losing, which all started when my husband fell ill.

I suffered because I couldn't get what I wanted, feared losing my husband, and complained bitterly about the years of hard work and sacrifice I put into our family.

But finally, the heavy backdrop of all those years of pain and exhaustion has completely turned a page, and in its place, there is now only love and forgiveness.

The harm of wrong views is unimaginable because they have infiltrated every aspect of my life. I used to live entirely under their influence. If it weren't for my Master who taught me the true Buddhist view, I, as someone trapped in wrong views, would've ended up in the Avici Hell without even knowing why!

The root has been thawed, my body and mind have been set free, and I've been completely liberated from the bondage of family. The feeling of liberation is absolutely wonderful. Then I shifted from clinging to outer appearances to turning inward, and I realized that all these years, I hadn't truly practiced at all. I was just spinning around on the level of forms and appearances. Finally, I've turned this corner, and I'm truly happy.

Outside the mind, no thing dwells. Seek the Dharma within the mind! The mind, the mind, and there is nothing else. Keep going!

Blessing and Merit

FATHER'S SOUL HAS GONE TO THE HEAVENLY PATH

Today, a friend of mine donated money to print books because his father is critically ill—this act is truly commendable. Because the Truth is the bridge to Heaven; behind the Truth stand countless gods and Buddhas. To propagate the Truth is to rescue souls; to support the printing of the Truth is to make offerings to the gods and Buddhas. This intention and the concrete action can truly increase merit, and the merit gained from making offerings to the Buddhas can indeed deliver souls from suffering. I have personally experienced such matters, with firsthand experience and insight.

It was in 2011 when I first learned that supporting the printing of the Dharma could deliver departed souls.

A student told me this in those days, but I absolutely didn't believe it back then.

He had wanted to offer me cash as a donation, but I didn't accept it. Later, he used that money to print Dharma books instead.

Six months later, during the Qingming Festival, he visited the graves of his late parents to pay his respects.

After cleaning the burial site, he went to see several Buddhist monks he knew.

He asked them about the current state of his deceased parents.

He wished to do whatever he could to help their souls in the afterlife.

He knew several people with supernatural abilities—Taoist priests and also a few monastics.

At that time he didn't know who I was, so he didn't truly believe in my abilities.

He was learning from me while also studying with others.

He went to a Taoist priest and asked about the situation of

his deceased relative.

After observing the underworld, the priest asked him: "Have you performed any great acts of merit in the past six months? Why was your relative, within just a few months, delivered to the heavenly path by a sacred and mighty force?"

He didn't believe it, so he went to another person with supernatural abilities to take a look, and they saw the same thing.

Then he came to me to ask about his parents.

I've had the heavenly eye open since childhood, so I can see both the divine beings in the heavenly path and the souls in the underworld.

I saw that his loved ones were indeed in the third level of the heavenly path.

So I told him truthfully: his parents had been delivered to the third level of the heavenly path by a sacred and powerful force of merit.

But I didn't know that this powerful, sacred merit was connected to me.

After I finished explaining what I saw about his parents, he said in surprise: "All three of you said exactly the same thing.

Most importantly, even the level of the heavenly path my

parents went to—you all gave the same answer."

He reflected on his words and actions over the past six months:

He hadn't gone to temples to release life, donate funds, conduct a Water-Land Ceremony, or make offerings to monks.

All he had done was take the cash he had originally intended to offer me and use it to support the printing of my books.

He had done some proofreading work, and only occasionally shared the Truth with others.

Yet such a small and insignificant act of spreading the Dharma had, in the microcosm, manifested such inconceivable merit.

Hearing him recount his experience in person, I was slightly moved, but I didn't really take it to heart.

Because in the view of a practitioner, "blessing and merit" are only useful for ghosts.

Having devoted my entire life to the path of liberation in this lifetime, as an Awakened One, what use do I have for merit or blessing?

Caring about them only keeps a practitioner's mind trapped

within the cycle of birth and death.

So subconsciously, I reject, even resist the idea of merit and blessing.

Over the years, from time to time, I have heard of many people experiencing miracles through propagating the Dharma.

Combined with my own experiences—the process of transforming karma into blessing, and blessing into merit—I underwent a real change in the nature of the soul within the microcosm of body and mind.

Only then did I completely overturn my prejudice against blessing in my mental cognition.

THE CONSEQUENCES OF LACKING BLESSING AND MERIT

I have a friend from my hometown, who developed a strange illness starting at the age of 25.

He suffers from severe myasthenia gravis, living as if disabled.

From one end of the country to the other, he sought medical treatment everywhere, but nothing worked.

For decades, he hasn't been able to work or live normally.

An ordinary person's normal life is a luxury he could never afford.

With supernatural vision, I observed the microcosm of his life and saw that his merit and blessing had been completely exhausted.

In the microscopic realm, his negative karma was as vast as the ocean, with dark clouds covering the sky and leaving no trace of light.

Therefore, although in real life he came from a wealthy

family and owned several properties, his own direct experience was one of living worse than death.

In the course of life, when faced with unavoidable disasters—during times of crisis—the power of merit and blessing reveals itself to uphold our lives.

For those who lack merit, even the slightest hardship can cause their life to plummet dramatically, as if falling off a cliff.

And when they fall to rock bottom, there is no longer any chance of seeing the light again.

Yet those with deep merit, even when struck by sudden disasters or numerous hardships, where it seems they've lost everything—their family torn apart, their life filled with suffering,

are often able to swiftly turn danger into safety, and transform misfortune into blessing.

I've seen this happen too many times, and experienced it myself more times than I can count.

For ordinary people, merit and blessing are like a lifelong insurance policy purchased from the Tathagata.

You can't cash it out or turn it into daily necessities during ordinary times.

But in the face of a catastrophic disaster, when you combine your unwavering faith with the blessing you've accumulated through spreading the Dharma, you can invite the gods and Buddhas who protect you to redeem that spiritual "insurance policy."

THE ESSENCE OF BLESSING

The universe is the "knowing-awareness" recalling Spirit within the seeing-nature, projected by the distinctions of "seeing-nature" within the body-mind of all beings.

Knowing-awareness is the fallen "Spirit"; Spirit's memory of Heaven itself is reflected through the dreams of knowing-awareness, casting forth the distinctions of the "heart-mind's seeing-nature." Spirit is eternal, pure, peaceful, joyful, infinite, perfect, and blissful; Spirit is Heaven itself. And seeing-nature is the essence of the heart-mind; the distinctions projected by seeing-nature are the dreams of knowing-awareness—a memory and imitation of Spirit Heaven. The recollection and imitation of Heaven, reflected through seeing-nature, give rise to the seven great elements—namely earth, water, fire, wind, perception, consciousness, and space—which constitute all things in the universe.

The universe arises from mind-consciousness; the world and the self arise from the distinctions of seeing-nature.

The world is but a manifestation of the mind; fate is but karmic causes and conditions, that are manifested through distinctions of the seen within seeing-nature.

Now, let's take a look at what humans call "blessing."

What humans consider as blessing is wealth, status, and respect from others;
these correspond to the abundance, perfection, and wholeness of Spirit Heaven.

Physical health, radiant beauty, a life of ease, and the fulfillment of all desires—these correspond to Life in Heaven expressing its love through forms of light: pure, stainless, free, and infinite.

Eternal youth, a harmonious family, a house full of children, and a successful career—these correspond to the eternal wholeness of Heaven, where eternal happiness and infinite bliss abide.

Endless wealth, renowned fame, a distinguished status, a life free from disasters and hardships, a long and venerable lifespan—these correspond to the infinite and boundless happiness, peace, abundance, and fulfillment in Heaven, where all wishes come true.

Humans cannot perceive the Spirit Realm.

Therefore, they cannot directly and personally experience the vast, profound difference between the human world and Heaven.

Yet I dwell in Heaven at every moment, in every place; the subject of experience at the core of this body—that is, the "inside" of the mind's seeing-nature—is the Spirit light of Heaven; thus, I am one with Heaven, and the Three Realms.

For the practitioner, Heaven and the Six Paths are fully and holistically present in an instant, in a holographic and multi-dimensional form.

The practitioner can see the informational content of the mind-heart that constitutes the "ego"-personality in this lifetime.

I see, within the arising of the "self"-mind, the countless subtle memories and habits embedded deep within every single thought.

I see the countless and varied forms of the "self"—arising within the endlessly subtle dimensional worlds, evolved through conditions and causes, moved by the flow of past and future time, existing in the boundless karmic realms, where karmic habits drive deliberating thought, following the continuum of cause and effect, within the deeply layered and profound microcosm, all connected to deliberating memory of the mind.

Beneath the conceptual "I" in mind-consciousness, lies not only the informational content of individual will, but also, interconnected with it, the vast and boundless system of the Three Realms and Six Paths—the entire cycle of samsaric birth and death.

Currently, the practitioner is liberated from the realm of individual will;

through primordial Life's Spirit radiance in wholeness, illuminating the Six Paths, shining upon the Spirit Realm, and simultaneously upon the human world within the Three Realms.

I know in detail the similarities and differences between the human world and Heaven.

Heaven is none other than Spirit—it is the primordial essence of Life, the Source of all souls; to put it differently, the true Self of every being originates from Heaven. In other words, sentient beings have strayed from Heaven, and the self that is lost and in fear, projects the "nightmare" of the human world.

Within human nature lie the qualities of Heaven. These heavenly qualities, extracted and expressed through human conduct, are purity and selflessness, integrity and justice, light and warmth, forgiveness and devotion, honesty and responsibility, as well as unconditional love and acceptance. Anyone—regardless of their status in the human world—whose state of heart-mind meets these essential criteria, has their inner being resonate with Heaven. Through the realm of their virtuous conduct, the light of Heaven will shine forth his body-mind, reflecting outward the flawless, eternal, and infinite radiance of the Spirit Realm. The light of the Spirit Heaven—when reflected through a human being on earth—manifests the infinite, the greatest and most fundamental blessing imaginable. That is the "perfect and eternal bliss."

In the most concise terms, summarize the essence of blessing: "True faith in the Divine or Buddha" awakens the innate goodness and warmth within the human heart. A heart willing to practice forgiveness and truthfulness will shine in harmony with the Spirit within body and mind. Spirit is Heaven itself. When a person follows faith, devotes to the Truth, and lives forgiveness and the warmth of love, the sacred light of Heaven will shine forth from within, illuminating their body, mind, and soul, nourishing their inner perception and sensation, purifying their conscious self, and gradually dissolving the karmic imprints that shape their personality.

Over time, although this person's body remains in the human world, their inner experience will abide eternally in the Heavenly state of warm peace, pure joy, subtle bliss, and radiant clarity. For a person whose heart is filled with light, radiant joy, and peaceful security, the conditions of earthly life truly do not matter. Whether you are rich or poor, healthy or ill, a beggar or a tycoon, your social status and living conditions will not in the least affect the bliss of your inner Heaven and the infinite happiness you feel within. Because what we call "life" in the real world is, fundamentally, a projection cast by the discriminating activity of mind-consciousness: namely, the memory held by the heart-mind's seeing-nature of the distinctions it makes about the seen. And seeing-nature originates from Spirit's memory of Heaven. When the memory of Heaven awakens within the heart's experience, the mental traces of earthly thoughts will be dispersed by the light of Spirit's memory of Heaven from the depths of the heart. Therefore, no matter where you are, the radiance of the Spirit Heaven cannot be swayed by the human mind-consciousness.

This is the fundamental source of all blessings.

In the end, what is true blessing for humanity?
It is the longing for Heaven, devotion to the Truth,
and the choice of the Divine and the Buddhas.

It has the power to alter destiny;
To bestow divine grace;
To breathe life into the dead;
To restore youth;
To avert calamities and dissolve suffering;
To grant entry into Heaven and
ultimate liberation from the cycle of birth and death.

The Difference Between Blessing and Merit

I was startled when I saw the true nature of this person's soul-microcosm.

Originally a desolate abyss of dried-up cliffs, where yellow sand stretched as far as the eye could see, now stood a towering, golden mountain range that soared into the clouds and was resplendent and magnificent.

It was as if, rising up from the depths of the Mariana Trench, there appeared the Himalayas, except this mountain was made entirely of gold. The golden mountain radiated with dazzling, brilliant beams of light, its countless rays of golden radiance illuminating the entire realm where the soul resides.

The golden peak stretched high into Heaven, piercing the very sky,

its summit reaching tens of thousands of meters into the air.

Clouds at great heights drifted around the middle slopes of

the golden mountain.

Upon carefully observing the changes within her soul's world, I was truly astonished and left speechless. I have encountered so many people in this human realm who are blessed with great worldly fortune. These individuals have either accumulated merit and blessing from practicing virtue and doing good deeds in past lives, or they have gathered virtuous karma and blessing through spiritual practice in this lifetime. Within the microscopic world of their being, where the soul resides, this blessing manifests as vast white clouds filling the void—like a season of abundant cotton harvests in Xinjiang, with soft, fluffy mounds of cotton spread across the open wilderness and desert plains. Blessing manifests as white, small hills, much like stacked cotton bales.

And yet, within the world behind this person's soul, there stood a golden mountain.

This was not the power of blessing. This was the power of merit.

If one were to put it into terms of exchange, even ten billion tons of cotton-bale blessing could not be traded for even one microgram of golden merit.

Because merit and blessing are substances that belong to different dimensions of space. Blessing is only accessible to beings within the energy universe, while merit is a form of provision that can only be attained by stepping into the Spirit Realm.

It's a bit like the contrast between light and soil, which is not merely a difference in form or density, but a fundamental difference in nature.

Ordinary beings in the human world who possess great blessing may use it to obtain glory, wealth, and honor; when disaster strikes, they turn misfortune into good fortune; they enjoy health, long life, and a house full of descendants. After living out their life in splendor, the soul carries the remaining blessing into reincarnation, taking birth in different favorable realms. With a mundane mind, they continue the cycle of birth and death—until their blessing is exhausted and they fall into the evil paths, assuming the form of hungry ghosts or animals to repay the ego-clinging karma created by the "discriminating activity of mind-consciousness."

As for a soul that possesses merit: because merit cannot be converted into blessing—merit is the provision that only divine beings possess, such a soul will not manifest as having self-indulgent glory and splendor in the human world.

On the contrary, because this soul has attained the qualification to become a divine being, the person will certainly undergo the process of "purifying" Spirit from within their mind-nature.

■ The soul of this person, after enduring countless blows, tramplings, ravages, and devastations in the human world,
still does not waver in its faith in "forgiveness,"
and still embraces the world with the warmth of holy love.
Still, with the warmth and kindness of love, it faces the darkness of human nature.
Still, with faith in forgiveness, it warms the evil that has harmed her.

Cases
REBIRTH AFTER THREE BANKRUPTCIES

Let me tell you about my true experience over the past thirteen years. If it weren't for meeting my Master and encountering the Truth, I would have been utterly lost beyond redemption.

In 2011, my husband ventured into futures trading and ended up losing approximately 10 million RMB. That was our first bankruptcy. I was 24 years old at the time, and he was 28.

Between 2014 and 2015, we finally managed to earn a significant amount of money, approximately 100 million RMB. But unexpectedly, that entire 100 million was completely wiped out. To cover the losses, we sold two properties, but it still wasn't enough, and we were left entirely insolvent. That was our second bankruptcy.

Our third bankruptcy came in 2022, when my husband

invested in pharmaceutical stocks, which turned out to be a failure. We lost roughly another 50 million RMB.

These were the three major bankruptcies in our lives and were the most significant ones. As for the other smaller or medium-scale investment failures, I won't bother going into detail. To be precise, we were in a state of bankruptcy for a full twelve years.

For years, I suffered from insomnia, anxiety, depression, and auditory hallucinations, symptoms that haunted me like shadows relentlessly. I became dependent on psychiatric medication just to function, living a life without any hope, a life that felt like hell on earth, where every single day felt worse than death.

A few years ago, I stumbled upon Master's articles online purely by chance, and then, incredibly, I came across Master's audio teachings as well. From that moment on, the gears of my destiny began to turn...

Since encountering the Truth, I haven't spent a single day without Master's voice.

Gradually, I found that my heart no longer raced outward in restless seeking.

I came to understand that seeking the Truth outside the mind is like trying to cook rice in sand, which is futile and empty. Little by little, a sense of security grew stronger within me. The oppression I once felt began to fade, and my struggles with insomnia and other symptoms gradually improved. Master taught us about forgiveness and and love, emphasizing forgiveness without definition, and love without distinction. To warm the self with love, to embrace the self with love, to forgive the self with love, and to accept everything with love.

As my heart healed and my body gradually regained its health, I began sharing Master's writings and audio teachings with many others who were lost and searching.

The more I shared, the more joy I felt. The more I shared, the more transformation I witnessed, both in myself and in others. At the same time, my husband's career also began to turn around. Our debts slowly started to shrink, and in just a few short years, we had paid off the huge amount of debt that we once thought we would never, ever be able to repay in this lifetime.

Now, I feel deeply happy within. Every day, I live with a relaxed, peaceful, and tranquil mind and body, and I am truly abundant both in spirit and in material well-being.

It was Master who saved my life. It was Master who completely reshaped my existence. The Master is none other than my second set of parents, who are my spiritual mother and father. Without Master, we would be no different from wandering ghosts trapped in hell. I am deeply grateful to for showing us: The root of all suffering is forgetting love. Only a soul that has lost love knows fear. Only a fearful heart lashes out at others. Forgive the parts of yourself that seem "unforgivable." Awaken love, and you will be redeemed by divine love.

Only love can melt away pain. The light of love has the power to heal the cells of the body, the mind, and the spirit.

Warm yourself with love, embrace yourself with love, forgive yourself with love, and accept everything with love.

Cases

I EARNED 10 TIMES MORE WITHOUT LEAVING HOME

Five years ago, my body was weak and fragile. There were so many things I couldn't do—I couldn't eat this, I couldn't drink that. I couldn't play games. I couldn't watch movies. What most people consider an ordinary, everyday life was nothing but a luxury to me. And that was the sign of the absence of blessings.

At the same time, due to my physical condition, I was unable to work a regular job and had to remain unemployed at home. Watching the balance in my bank account dwindle day by day, I often felt anxious and fearful about my future. I thought about selling small items online to make ends meet, but even that brought in only a meager income each month.

Later, as I began to study the Truth, I started to turn my life around by following Master's guidance to practice forgiveness and promote the Dharma. The anxiety and fear that once filled my heart were gradually melted away by love and warmth.

Little by little, I could feel that my life was beginning to improve, and my blessings were gradually accumulating. Then, last year, a job that was both easy and well-suited to me came to me, and I did not even have to go out to find it. In recent months, my monthly income has reached about ten times what it used to be.

Now, life has become much more comfortable and I can buy whatever I want.

But the richness I feel inside isn't about having a lot of material things. It's a sense of inner abundance, which is a feeling that nothing is missing, that there's no tension, no anxiety, no worry about the future. I feel at ease, comfortable, and truly happy, in a state of lacking nothing and needing nothing more.

This is what it means for blessing to arise, and it turns out that blessing is reflected not only in material wealth, but even more so in the state of our inner being. All of this is a blessing and gift from the Truth. Devotion to the Truth brings me a profound sense of warmth and happiness.

I have a friend who comes from a well-off, middle-class family and is the kind of person who has everything materially. Yet, when it comes to his work and business, things just don't go smoothly. He's constantly worried about the future, and when we talk, I can clearly sense the emptiness, anxiety, and unease within him. That's what it means to lack blessing.

A person with sufficient blessing may not have much materially right now, yet they don't feel a sense of lack within. They have an inner certainty that what they need will come in time, and as a result, they experience little anxiety and seldom worry.

Expel a Spirit

ALL TYPES OF POSSESSION CAN BE HEALED

Student: (During the possession) Back then, I felt extremely weak and drained, and I was mentally foggy, as if my very life force was being slowly drained away. I was filled with inner fear, but driven by my will to survive and my faith in Master's Teachings, I kept studying the teachings, copying the sacred texts, and holding on. Gradually, I began to recover and stabilize. Now, my practice is sometimes diligent, sometimes lax, but my faith has grown firmer and more certain. I will follow Master and cultivate myself for life.

I still have questions I want answered: Is there really such a thing as possession?

Animals lack reason, discipline, and moral concepts. An animal spirit endowed with extraordinary powers will certainly—and is destined to—corrupt the human world and harm humanity.

If so, what kind of beings are involved? And will they harm the world in the future? (Excerpt)

Master: The entire Three Realms and Six Paths, in the eyes of the sages of the Dharma Realm, are like a single grain of sand on the fingertip; amid countless kalpas of birth and death, the endless karmic obstacles and boundless darkness endured by sentient beings are, in the eyes of the True Divine, merely dust resting in the palm of a hand—not worth mentioning.

What makes humans turn pale at the mention of "possession" is, in the Sanctuary, merely a microorganism. What causes religious followers to tremble and panic at the rumor of demons and monsters is, in the Sanctuary, nothing but mites.

These scourges that plague the human world are, to the true practitioners, not even worth discussing, as they are but a joke.

Listen to my audio and live by it. No matter what kind of possession you may have, you will heal completely—one hundred percent. As long as your soul abides with the Truth, no evil spirit or demonic force can ever intimidate you. I guarantee this.

The Truth has the power to deliver souls to Heaven, and what kind of might is this?

The Truth can bring the dead back to life, so what kind of miracle is this?

Possession, vengeful spirits, and ghosts—in the instant your heart-mind resonates with the Truth, are all bathed in the holy light of the Dharma Realm.

They will either be liberated by the Light of compassion,

or extinguished by the supreme Divine power—it depends on their own choice.

Divine beings are fundamentally different from humans. Never use your petty mindset of human beings to speculate about the compassion and awe-inspiring power of the True Divine. As long as your heart and wishes abide in faith, no being in the Three Realms can ever threaten you.

For faith abides with the Buddhas.

Student: Looking back over the past three months of studying the Dharma, I feel that the previous attachments from heterodox influences are still with me, disturbing me and hindering my practice.

Master: Wear your headphones and listen to my teachings 24 hours a day. Go through all the audio recordings, as doing so can completely heal the possessions within you. While listening, hold this intention in your heart: "My Master's voice is my true thought. Any other thoughts are not mine." In this way, you open your heart and let the True Divine dwell within your heart-mind; then the light of the True Divine will dispel the low-level entities within you.

Cases

Demonic possession of "dual cultivation" cleared away

Between 2018 and 2019, I encountered two false teachers: one was a demonic figure promoting "slapping therapy," and the other was a false Master who claimed to be from the Vajrayana (Tantric) tradition. Due to my deep ignorance and heavy karmic obstacles, I engaged in so-called "dual cultivation" with both of these demonic beings. For a long time afterward, I suffered greatly under the possession and interference of evil spirits sent by the false Vajrayana Master. The torment was unbearable.

During the time I was involved with that false teacher, there was one occasion when I was taking a bath and my body began to feel an abnormal, intense heat. For a short while, I even felt as if a long, grotesque tongue was writhing and sweeping inside my belly. On another day, out of nowhere, I suddenly felt freezing cold, with a splitting headache, vomiting and diarrhea at the same time, and completely drained of strength.

The possessed man—if you engage in so-called "dual cultivation" with him, your soul will be utterly ruined. He is not just some dirty pervert or ordinary sex criminal. He is a demonic entity that feeds on human essence and blood.

The symptoms lasted from noon until 6 p.m., and then, just as suddenly and inexplicably, they vanished completely, as if nothing had happened. When I sent a WeChat message asking him about it, he simply replied: "I missed you." Later on, similar episodes happened several more times, and each time, it turned out he was indulging in lustful thoughts about me. He once even made gestures over my abdomen as if drawing a talisman or spell, all while muttering incantations under his breath.

I officially began transcribing the teachings in October 2020. Two months later, karmic obstacles began to emerge. On weekends, the false teacher's side would frequently harass me. I would experience dizziness, a tightening sensation around my temples as if a tight band were being cinched around my head, and at times, an excruciating headache as if my skull were splitting apart. My body would grow cold, sometimes accompanied by vomiting and diarrhea. The pain was so severe that I could hardly move. Often, I could only lie semi-reclined all day long, barely able to function, and it felt like living hell.

At one point, the pain became so unbearable that I actually thought of pleading with him to let me go. But the moment that thought arose, I could feel his anger and humiliation directed straight at me. Later, I blocked and deleted all of his contact information, and completely distanced myself from him.

Those kinds of days went on intermittently for as long as four months. If it weren't for my Master's compassionate salvation, if it weren't for the purification by the Truth, and if it weren't for my simple, unwavering faith, I truly can't imagine how I could have endured those days.

Since studying the Truth, I haven't been to a hospital even once, nor have I taken a single painkiller. On the rare occasions when the pain became unbearable, I would pour menthol oil all over my head, and continuously massage and tap the area. At the same time, I listened to the teachings, listened to *Dream* day and night, and I never dared to be apart from my Master's voice, not even for a moment.

Master once gave the following instruction to a fellow practitioner: "When you entrust your soul completely and without reservation to the True Divine, the attachments will be cleared away by the Dharma Protectors, and your life will be redeemed by Heaven."

And indeed, it was just as Master said. After following the teachings for two years, those feelings of being disturbed by spiritual entities completely disappeared.

My body has grown stronger and healthier with each passing day, my skin is glowing, my eyes are bright, and my entire being radiates a youthful, vibrant energy.

My heart has also become softer and more open. Truly, I have been completely reborn, like a phoenix rising from the ashes.

Cases

A YOUTH WAS POSSESSED BY AN EVIL SPIRIT

My son has a good friend who was studying in Belarus. When this young man returned to China and came to our home for a meal one day, I noticed something unusual about his body the moment he walked in: his head would involuntarily nod every few seconds. My intuition immediately told me that he was possessed by an entity.

Then I quickly gave him the small and the large audio players containing my Master's Teachings.

I instructed him to wear the small one on him at all times, never taking it off, and to keep the large one playing continuously in the living room..

Later, the young man shared that on the very first night he brought the devices home, he finally had a peaceful sleep. Before that, ever since returning to China, he had been having nightmares every night, which were dreams about his

Being possessed by demonic forces is, in essence, a state in which one loses rational control over consciousness. Instead, one's emotional impulses and desires take over, manipulating the mind and giving rise to various forms of mental illness, such as schizophrenia, mania, dissociative identity disorder, and delusional disorders.

grandfather who had passed away not long ago.

The young man truly benefited from the Dharma audio player. He became very conscientious about carrying the small one with him and never dared to go without it. One evening, when he and my son were out playing, he proudly patted his pocket and asked, "Did you bring yours? I've got mine!" My son

later told me, "He plays the device really loud. He says it keeps those things around him from getting close."

Before the young man returned to Belarus, he and his mother came to our home for a meal again. This time, I could hardly notice those involuntary head nods anymore.

His mother shared that after she first noticed her son's

nodding, she had taken him to the hospital, but the doctors found nothing wrong and said everything was normal. She had never been a religious person before, but this time, she truly experienced the power of the Dharma audio player. After returning home, she took the large device and started playing it in her own bedroom.

Not long ago, a fellow Buddhist practitioner invited me to visit a young woman, only 20 years old, at the local psychiatric hospital. It was said that this was already her third episode, and the hospital had diagnosed her with depression. As soon as we saw her, we shared with her various real-life cases of people who had benefited from our Master's Teachings. At the same time, we hung a small Dharma audio player around her neck, playing *Dream* on repeat.

Just a few minutes later, the young woman suddenly said, "Auntie, it really works!"

I was puzzled and asked, "What works?" She replied, "This device works. My hallucinations are gone!" We were surprised and asked, "What? You've been hearing things too?" She answered, "Yes. Usually, I feel like there are so many people talking right into my ear. It's so annoying. But the moment I put on this little device, those voices just disappear!" Wow, that was incredible. Before leaving the hospital, I reminded her to wear the small device 24 hours a day, except when she needed to use the restroom.

The next day, I messaged her on WeChat and asked if she had slept well the night before. She told me that ever since she started wearing the small Dharma device, she had finally slept soundly—and she was so happy about it. Before that, aside from the auditory hallucinations, she had also suffered from chronic insomnia. Even while hospitalized and on medication, she couldn't sleep at all.

Another four or five days later, I asked her again how she had been sleeping recently.

She replied cheerfully, "I'm sleeping really well!" She felt that she was ready to be discharged from the hospital this time. I encouraged her to continue listening to the Dharma around the clock, even after going home.

Life has never left love

All souls belong to love

Love has forgotten no one

Audio

Video

YouTube

Spotify

Contast us

WhatsApp

LINE

The Everlasting Answer—Love

Paperback ISBN: 978-1-923572-33-1

Ebook ISBN: 978-1-923572-34-8

Published by De Fu Publishing

1st edition, 2026

Website: www.defupublishing.com

E-mail: info@defupublishing.com

Price : AUD $38.99

www.ingramcontent.com/pod-product-compliance
Lightning Source LLC
LaVergne TN
LVHW051132210926
848482LV00001B/71
9781923572331